Games for All Ages

100 Fun Activities Everyone Can Play

Group LOVELAND, COLORADO

Group's R.E.A.L. Guarantee to you:

Every Group resource incorporates our R.E.A.L. approach to ministry—a unique philosophy that results in long-term retention and life transformation. It's ministry that's:

This is EARL. He's R.E.A.L. mixed up. (Get it?)

Relational
Because student-to-student interaction enhances learning and builds Christian friendships.

Experiential
Because what students experience sticks with them up to 9 times longer than what they simply hear or read.

Applicable
Because the aim of Christian education is to be both hearers and doers of the Word.

Learner-based
Because students learn more and retain it longer when the process is designed according to how they learn best.

GAMES FOR ALL AGES
100 Fun Activities Everyone Can Play

Visit our Web site: **www.grouppublishing.com**

Credits
Contributing Authors: Katrina Arbuckle, Tim Baker, Michael W. Capps, Steve Case, Monica Kay Glenn, Stacy Haverstock, Michele Howe, Trish Kline, Pamela Ann Malloy, Teresa McCasland, Julie Meiklejohn, Todd Outcalt, Christina Schofield, Donna K. Stearns
Editor: Amy Simpson
Creative Development Editor: Jim Kochenburger
Chief Creative Officer: Joani Schultz
Copy Editor: Dena Twinem
Art Director: Jean Bruns
Designers: Suzanne Nelson, Jean Bruns
Computer Graphic Artist: Nancy Serbus
Illustrator: Jessica Wolk-Stanley
Cover Art Director: Jeff A. Storm
Cover Designer: Blukazoo Studio
Cover Illustrator: Laura Cornell
Production Manager: Dodie Tipton

Unless otherwise noted, Scripture taken from the HOLY BIBLE, NEW INTERNA-TIONAL VERSION®. Copyright © 1973, 1978, 1984 by International Bible Society. Used by permission of Zondervan Publishing House. All rights reserved.

Library of Congress Cataloging-in-Publication Data
Games for All Ages - 100 Fun Activities Everyone Can Play
     p. cm.
   ISBN 0-7644-2216-2 (alk. paper)
   1. Church work with families. 2. Games in Christian education. 3. Church group work with teenagers. I. Group Publishing.

BV4438 .F334 2001
259'.1--dc21

                                                                                    2001016103

10 9 8 7 6 5 4 3 2   11 10 09 08 07 06 05 04 03 02
Printed in the United States of America.

Contents

SECTION 4:

Games With a Point

Introduction

Finally—a collection of group games for your ministry, all suitable for family and intergenerational events! You can play the fun games in this book in your youth ministry, at adult fellowship gatherings, or at all-church events! These games are designed to bring generations together—from preteens to seniors, these one hundred games really *are* fun for all ages!

This book includes four types of games: high-action games, low-key games, get-to-know-you games, and games with a point. The games involve a variety of physical activity levels to appeal to people of different ages and energy levels. The games also use creative (yet practical) supplies and fresh ideas to make for a unique collection of fun activities.

Use these games to help people in your church get to know each other and to spark important discussions. Use them to draw families closer together and to promote discussion between parents and their children. *Games for All Ages* provides fun ways to help players grow as they're having fun!

High-Action GAMES

Alphabet Bible Race

DESCRIPTION: Participants will race to write names from the Bible on poster board. The first team to get through Z wins.

SUPPLIES: poster board, markers, two Bibles

Before the game, hang two pieces of poster board on a wall in your meeting area. Place a marker and a Bible next to each piece of poster board. Use masking tape or chalk to mark a starting line about ten feet away from the poster board.

Have participants form two equal teams. Instruct each team to stand behind the starting line. Explain that the first person in line from each team will race to that team's poster board and write down a name from the Bible that starts with A. That person will then run back to the starting line, and the second person in line will run down and write a Bible name that starts with B. Teammates may confer to come up with Bible names for all the letters.

When the teams are ready, tell them to start. The first team to make it through Z is the winner.

Around the World

DESCRIPTION: Put on your running shoes; this is no ordinary Ping-Pong game.

SUPPLIES: Ping-Pong table, Ping-Pong ball, two Ping-Pong paddles

Have players form two groups. Place each group in a single file line at one end of the Ping-Pong table, and give the Ping-Pong ball to one group. The first player in line in that group will serve the Ping-Pong ball, quickly lay his or her paddle on the table, and run to the end of the line on the opposite side of the table. The player on the opposite side of the table should be prepared to hit the ball once, as in a regular Ping-Pong game, and then put the paddle on the table and run to the end of the line on the opposite side of the table. In other words, each player hits the ball once, lays down the paddle, and runs to the end of the line on the opposite side of the table.

The next person in line on each end must quickly pick up the paddle to keep the game going by repeating this same sequence. If a ball is hit off the table, the person who hit it is out of the game. If the recipient misses the ball or fails to hit it back over the net, that person is out.

The game continues until only one person is left.

Attached Relay

DESCRIPTION: Partners will run a relay while tied back to back.

SUPPLIES: table, crackers, two pitchers of water, cups, bubble gum, yarn, scissors

Before this game, set up a table at one end of your meeting area. On the table, set out two piles of crackers, two pitchers of water, two stacks of cups, and two piles of bubble gum.

Have players form two groups. Have the players in each group form pairs. Ask partners to stand back to back as you tie their ankles, arms, and wrists to each other. To make this go faster, you many want to enlist the help of pairs who haven't yet been tied together.

When partners are tied together, encourage them to practice moving and walking around for a few minutes. Then instruct pairs to get back in their two larger groups. Have each group form a straight line, one pair behind another, facing the table at the other end of the meeting area.

Game Leader TIP

IT'S A GOOD IDEA TO HAVE A COUPLE OF VOLUNTEERS STANDING AT THE TABLE READY TO REFILL THE WATER PITCHERS AND TO MAKE SURE PLAYERS FILL THEIR CUPS ALL THE WAY.

Explain that the first pair in each line must walk as quickly as possible to the table. Once there, partners must feed each other a cracker. Then each partner must fill a cup with water and give it to his or her partner (each person must drink a whole cup). Then each person must open a piece of chewing gum and feed it to his or her partner. Finally, each person must blow a bubble.

After the pair has completed all the tasks, the pair

moves quickly to the back of the team's line, and the next pair in line hurries to the table.

Repeat this process until each pair has completed all the tasks at the table. The first team whose pairs have finished the table challenge wins.

Baby's Bedtime

DESCRIPTION: Everyone will love this hilarious relay race to get "the baby" ready for bed.

SUPPLIES: three tables; water; diapers; two each: rocking chairs, cribs or cradles, baby bottles, baby bathtubs, towels, baby dolls

Before this game, set up three tables in a line across the room, followed by two rocking chairs and two cribs or cradles. The three tables are stations one, two, and three; the rocking chairs are station four; and the cribs or cradles are station five. The farther you can spread out these stations, the funnier the game will be. On the first table, set out two baby bottles. On the second table, set two baby bathtubs filled with water and two towels. On the third table, set a stack of diapers.

Have participants form two teams. Start the game with a player from each team at each station. If you have more than five players per team, the extra players should stand in line behind station one and wait for their turns.

To start the game, give the first player on each team a baby doll. That player must "feed" the baby, then "burp" the baby by patting it on the back twenty times. Player one then tosses the doll to the next player at station two. That person must wash and dry the baby, then toss the doll to the player at station three. The third player must put a diaper on the baby and then pass the baby to the player at station four, who must sit in the rocking chair and sing "Rock-a-Bye Baby" to the doll, then toss the baby to player five. When the player at station five receives the baby, he or she must put the baby in the crib or cradle, kneel, and pray the "Now I Lay Me Down to Sleep" prayer.

After player five says "amen," he or she runs to the front of the line with the baby. Each player then moves down one station, and an extra player enters the game if necessary. The game is complete when every player has had a chance to perform at each station.

Beach Ball Relay

DESCRIPTION: Players race each other with a ball between their knees, then pass the ball to teammates without using their hands.

SUPPLIES: tape or chalk, inflated beach ball for each team, sunglasses for each team

Before the game, use tape or chalk to mark a starting line and a finish line at least ten feet apart.

Have participants form teams of three and take off their shoes. Teams should stand behind the starting line. Give each team a beach ball and a pair of sunglasses.

One person on each team should put on the sunglasses and place the beach ball between his or her knees. When the game begins, that person races to the finish line and back to the starting line, where he or she must hand off the sunglasses to a teammate and pass the ball without the use of any hands. Each team member should take a turn racing to the finish line and back with the beach ball and sunglasses.

Brady Boggle

DESCRIPTION: This is a zany game of matching characters from *The Brady Bunch*.

SUPPLIES: blindfolds

Have players scatter throughout the playing area. Have each person put on a blindfold. Then assign each player the name of one of *The Brady Bunch* kids (Greg, Marcia, Peter, Jan, Bobby, Cindy). It's OK to repeat names as much as necessary. If you want to, you can also add in Mike, Carol, Alice, and Tiger.

When you begin the game, the Bradys will have to find each other by screaming out the names of the characters they've been assigned. No one can speak any other words.

There are several ways to play this game:

- All Gregs must find each other, all Marcias, all Cindys, and so on.

- A "Greg" must find a "Marcia," a "Peter" must find a "Jan," and so on. Once a team has paired up, no other Brady kid may join that pair. (Note: In order to do this, you must be sure you've assigned the names evenly.)

- This one is for large groups. Players must put together full Brady "families." When a group has "somehow formed a family," they may yell out, "Brady Bunch!"

Bubbly Softball

DESCRIPTION: Your group will have slip-sliding fun with softball—great for a hot day!

SUPPLIES: four baby swimming pools, four long strips of plastic such as heavy-duty trash bags cut into strips and taped together, dish soap, softball, bat

This game should be played outdoors on grass or dirt, since slipping and sliding is part of the fun. Before the game, create a softball diamond by placing baby swimming pools at home plate, first base, second base, and third base. Place the plastic strips between home and first, first and second, second and third, and third and home.

Fill the pools with water and make bubbles with the dish soap, hose down the plastic, and add dish soap to make it a little slippery. Have participants form two teams and play ball, using regular softball rules.

Candy Manipulation

DESCRIPTION: Partners will follow a path while holding a peppermint stick between their teeth.

SUPPLIES: construction paper, scissors, tape, peppermint sticks, red string licorice.

Before the game, cut construction paper into the shapes of candies. Tape these paper candies on the floor to form a path from one end of the room to the other. Create three paths of different colors so each team can travel on its own path. Paths can intersect at points.

Have players form three teams, and have the players on each team form pairs. Give each pair a peppermint stick. Instruct the teams to allow only one pair at a time on its "candy path."

Before you begin the game, station yourself at the end of the room where the paths end, and be ready to hand out red string licorice.

Members of each pair will place the peppermint stick in their mouths (with each person holding an end between his or her teeth). Partners must travel their path without dropping their stick. When they reach the end of the path, each partner must take a piece of licorice and tie it onto the peppermint stick while still holding the peppermint stick in his or her mouth. Partners must have two pieces of licorice tied onto the peppermint stick before they can travel back down their path to the beginning. If they drop the peppermint stick out of their mouths while tying the licorice, they must start over at the beginning.

Once the first pair has completed the path, the next pair of players begins. After the entire team has traveled the path and is back at the beginning, the game ends. The first team whose players successfully travel the path and tie the licorice onto their peppermint sticks wins.

Cats and Dogs

DESCRIPTION: Players will use flashlights to tag anyone with an animal shape on his or her body.

SUPPLIES: paper shapes of dogs and cats, tape, flashlights

Before the game, make sure your playing area can be completely darkened. Also, make sure the playing area is nice and big—you'll need plenty of room to run around.

Have players form two groups. Hand out flashlights to one entire group. If you don't have enough flashlights, have that group form pairs, and give one flashlight to each pair. Give the other team paper shapes of dogs and cats, and have them tape the shapes anywhere on their clothing, as long as they're visible—not hidden under collars or sleeve cuffs, for example.

Once the dog-and-cat group is ready, establish boundaries for the game. Explain to both groups that you'll be turning off the lights. When you say "go," the team with the flashlights must try to shine their lights on dog or cat people.

Both groups should keep moving around the playing area. The dog-and-cat people should move in an effort not to be caught with flashlights shining on their animal shapes. The flashlight group tries to catch the dogs and cats. Once a flashlight player spots a dog or a cat, he or she can put that dog or cat "out" by tagging it with the beam of his or her flashlight. Then the tagged dog or cat player must give the flashlight player the animal shape.

Allow players five minutes for the game. At the end of five minutes, each team should count its total number of cats and dogs. The team with the most dogs and cats wins the game.

Centipede Race

DESCRIPTION: Participants will work closely to win a race in this fun version of the old standard three-legged race.

SUPPLIES: two-foot length of rope or twine for each player, masking tape or chalk

Before the game, use tape or chalk to mark two lines on the floor about fifteen feet apart. Set half the pieces of rope or twine next to each line.

Have participants form two equal teams. Ask half of each team to stand behind each line (see the diagram on the next page).

Have each team choose two participants on one side to go first. The participants should stand side by side and use one piece of rope or twine to tie one person's left leg to the other person's right leg.

Explain that when you say "go," the first two participants will run to the other line. One participant on the other side will stand next to one of the first two participants and tie his or her leg to the leg of that participant. The three will then run back to the first line and "pick up" another teammate.

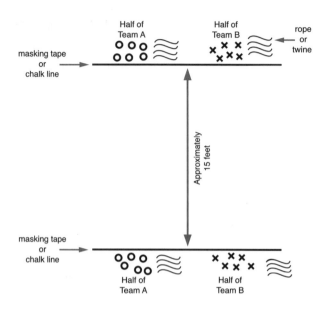

Continue the race in this manner until teams have crossed the finish line with all their members attached to each other.

Circle Up

DESCRIPTION: Participants will attempt to remain part of a circle.

SUPPLIES: none

Begin the game by inviting everyone to form circles consisting of four people each. Participants should hold hands once their circles are formed. (If you have an odd number of people, you can begin with circles of five or six.)

One person should stand outside the circles. This person will begin the game as the "Caller," but must be ready to join a circle whenever he or she calls, "Circle up!"

The Caller begins the game by giving instructions to the circles. Those within the circles must follow the instructions. For example, the Caller might say, "circle to the left," "circle to the right," or "lock arms and kick your feet to the middle." Instructions that keep the circles moving work best.

Eventually the Caller will yell, "Circle up!" At this point, everyone in each circle must leave that circle and find another group of four. The Caller also goes into the mix and finds a circle. This will leave one person outside the circles. This person then becomes the new Caller, and the process repeats.

Double-Trouble Kickball

DESCRIPTION: This kickball game will frustrate and amuse your group as participants attempt to play kickball while attached to another person.

SUPPLIES: two-foot lengths of rope or twine (one for every two people), kickball, bases

This is a perfect game for a group that's too large to play regular kickball. Have players form two teams, then have team members form pairs. Give each pair a length of rope or twine, and have partners tie one person's left leg to the other person's right leg as if for a three-legged race.

A kicking pair can opt for either person to kick the ball or to use the pair's third leg. A pair fielding the ball can use either person's hands to pick up the ball and throw it. Other than these rules, all the rules are the same as regular kickball.

Find That Picture

DESCRIPTION: Four groups will compete with each other to find specific pictures from magazines and newspapers.

SUPPLIES: magazines, newspapers

Have participants form four groups. Have one group go to each corner of the room. Give each group a stack of magazines and newspapers, and stand in the middle of the room.

Once groups are ready, yell out a picture for them to find and bring to you. When one group has brought you that picture, call out another item. Continue until participants are tired of playing or their magazines and newspapers are all torn up.

Here are some ideas for pictures or text you might want to have teams look for.

- the letter m
- a picture of a politician
- a picture of an athlete
- a score of a game
- a picture of another country's leader
- a picture of a movie star
- a graph or chart
- the name of our town
- a famous person under the age of twenty

Find the Shades

DESCRIPTION: Players will use flashlights to find the person wearing sunglasses.

SUPPLIES: sunglasses (the funnier, the better), flashlights

Before this game, be sure you can completely darken the playing area. Have participants form two teams. Hand out flashlights to one team, and give the sunglasses to one person on the other team. Explain that you'll turn out the lights and the team with the flashlights will search for the person wearing the sunglasses. The team with the sunglasses will try to keep the glasses moving from one person to another. As soon as one person puts on the sunglasses, he or she can immediately take them off and pass them to another player on the team. Someone must always be wearing them, putting them on, or taking them off.

The team with the flashlights will try to spot the person with the sunglasses, then tag the person wearing them. If the player wearing the glasses is spotted, he or she still can remove them and pass them on before being tagged. Once a person is tagged, he or she must yell, "I'm out" and go stand at a designated spot in the playing area. Once three players are out, stop the game. Then have teams switch roles and play another round.

Fishing for People

DESCRIPTION: This fast-paced relay game will keep everyone moving.

SUPPLIES: fishing rods and reels, rubber practice weights for casting, cardboard boxes, chalk

This game works best for a large group and should be played outdoors. Before the game, mark a line on the ground with chalk.

Have players form teams of at least six people. Each team should station half its team members in a line behind the line you marked on the ground earlier. Give the first person in each line a fishing rod. The other half of each team should be stationed thirty to forty feet away, behind a cardboard box.

When the game begins, the first member of each team will begin trying to cast the rubber practice weight into the cardboard box stationed near the other team members. If the weight hits the box or goes in, one of the team members on the other end gets "reeled" to the other side. The team member should simply grab hold of the rubber weight and walk along as the other team member reels him or her in.

Once a team member has made a successful cast and catch, he or she should run to the other side near the box to be reeled in. The game continues until each person has made a successful "catch" and has been "caught." The first team to successfully catch all its team members wins.

Foursquare Volleyball

DESCRIPTION: This is volleyball with a unique twist. Participants will never know which direction the ball will come from!

SUPPLIES: at least one volleyball, two or four volleyball nets

Before the game, set up the volleyball nets. You can set up four volleyball nets or just use two, depending on the size of your group. Arrange the nets according to one of the diagrams below.

If you use two nets, form two right angles like this:

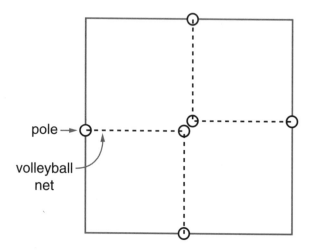

If you use four nets, fan the nets out from the center like this:

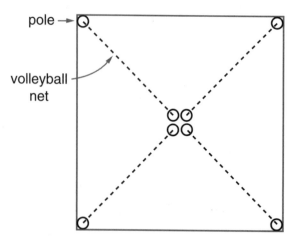

Have players form four teams. Assign each team one section of the volleyball court. Tell teams this game is played like regular volleyball, except they can hit the ball to any of the other sections.

To make the game even more interesting, start several volleyballs in different sections of the court.

Group Juggling

DESCRIPTION: Players work together to keep several paper balls in motion.

SUPPLIES: scrap paper

Before the game, crumple several pieces of scrap paper into balls. Have players form one group for every eight to ten people. Have players in each group stand in a circle about an arm's length apart. Players must stay in the circle, but they can move around within a three-foot radius of where they're standing to hit the balls.

Give each group three or four paper balls, and instruct groups to try to keep the papers in motion by continuously tossing them from one person to another. It helps to start one ball and get a rhythm going and then add in the other balls.

Hoop Loopers

DESCRIPTION: Participants will try to score points while defending their own hoops.

SUPPLIES: plastic hoops, foam balls

Have participants form teams of four, and give each team one hoop and one foam ball. The objective is to toss the ball into opponents' hoops while preventing them from scoring on your hoop.

Three team members will be hoop holders. At all times, they must keep both hands in contact with the hoop. The fourth person is the ball tosser and the only team member allowed to move about freely.

Once the game begins, all hoops must remain stationary except when the fourth team member places a hand on the hoop. When all four members are touching the hoop, they may move about freely. As soon as the tosser breaks away, the hoop must again remain stationary.

While the tosser is away, attempting to score on other teams' hoops, the three hoop holders must devise clever ways to divert would-be scorers. For example, they might shield the inside of the hoop by ducking their heads into it or by rotating it in place.

All teams should select a name and, when a point is scored, the tosser calls out his or her team's name and says a point has been scored. A scorekeeper will keep record and announce a winner when one team has scored seven points.

Indoor Obstacle Foam Softball

DESCRIPTION: In this unique softball game, players will find it difficult to hit a "home run" since pie tins dangling from the ceiling will obstruct the hit.

SUPPLIES: pie tins, string, chairs (optional), foam bat, foam ball

Before the game, hang pie tins at varying heights from the ceiling of the playing area. You can even add floor obstacles by leaving chairs in various places where they'll obstruct play.

Have participants form two teams and play a regular game of softball, dealing with the obstacles as they get in the way. If your group is too large for two teams, have them form three groups—while one group is at bat, another is the fielding team, and the third group becomes obstacles people must go around to run the bases.

This game can get crazy!

Lazy Foosball

DESCRIPTION: In this human foosball simulation, players will try to make goals for their teams, but they must remain seated in chairs.

SUPPLIES: beach ball, eighteen folding chairs

Before the game, set up chairs in a large open area as shown in the diagram below.

Have players form two teams, and place seven players from each team in position as illustrated. Each team's chairs should always face that team's goal. Extra players should sit on the sidelines, waiting to enter the game.

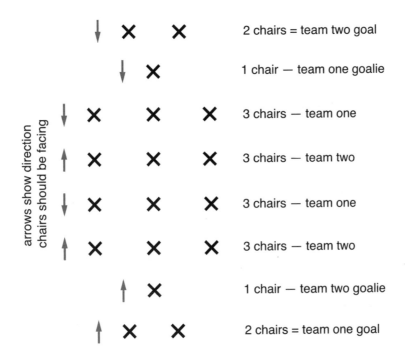

↓ X X	2 chairs = team two goal
↓ X	1 chair — team one goalie
↓ X X X	3 chairs — team one
↑ X X X	3 chairs — team two
↓ X X X	3 chairs — team one
↑ X X X	3 chairs — team two
↑ X	1 chair — team two goalie
↑ X X	2 chairs = team one goal

arrows show direction chairs should be facing

SAY:

Each team will attempt to make goals by hitting or kicking this beach ball through the two chairs at the opposite end of the room. Everyone must stay seated in his or her chair.

While the game is in progress, watch for and record goals and retrieve dead balls, tossing them back into play. Stop the game every few minutes to allow new players to substitute for the players on the field.

Name That Year

DESCRIPTION: This team runaround game includes a history lesson.

SUPPLIES: 51 pieces of paper, marker, tape

Before the game, write each year from 1950 to 1999 on its own piece of paper. Tape the signs in order along the walls of your playing area.

Gather players in the middle of the room. Be sure they know they can't move until you read a description of a historical event and say "go." Then they'll have five seconds to find and stand by the sign for the year they think that event happened.

Read aloud one of the items from the "Historical Events" list and say "go." After five seconds, award a point to the people who chose the correct year or came within one year on either side of the correct year.

Have players keep track of their points, and see who can get the most correct.

Historical Events
- The comic strip *Peanuts* debuts (1950)
- G.I. Joe debuts (1964)
- First climbers reach the top of Mount Everest (1953)
- Atari introduces "Pong" (1972)
- Medical association links smoking with lung cancer (1957)
- First man walks on the moon (1969)
- First copy machine is invented (1959)
- First video game is invented (1960)
- First McDonald's restaurant opens (1954)
- Prince Charles marries Lady Diana (1981)
- Berlin Wall construction begins (1961)
- Michael Jordan scores 20,000th career point (1993)
- Safety belts are introduced (1952)
- John F. Kennedy is assassinated (1963)

- The Bee Gees make their debut (1967)
- Legos are patented (1958)
- Post-It notes are created (1974)
- Martin Luther King is assassinated (1968)
- Dustin Hoffman wins an Academy Award for *Rain Man* (1988)
- Disneyland opens in California (1955)
- The first President Bush vomits on Japan's prime minister (1992)
- The Beatles debut (1962)
- First VCR is invented (1971)
- Federal Trade Commission declares Microsoft a monopoly (1999)
- Watergate scandal breaks in Washington (1973)
- First space walk (1965)
- A female astronaut goes into outer space for the first time (1983)
- The movie *Top Gun* premieres (1986)
- First personal computer is marketed (1975)
- First transatlantic hot-air balloon trip (1987)
- Viking I lands on Mars (1976)
- Nancy Kerrigan/Tonya Harding scandal makes the news (1994)
- The Beatles split up (1970)
- First *Star Wars* film debuts (1977)
- First Miss World Pageant (1951)
- Proof of living organisms discovered on a meteorite from Mars (1996)
- Gorbachev becomes leader of U.S.S.R. (1985)
- The movie *Superman* debuts (1978)
- "Star Trek" debuts on NBC (1966)
- Rollerblades and CDs are invented (1980)
- Rosanne divorces husband number three (1998)
- First artificial heart put into a human (1982)
- First successful cloning of mammal takes place (1997)
- Velcro is perfected for commercial use (1956)
- The Soviet Union ends (1991)
- The first astronaut flies in space *without* a safety line (1984)
- Exxon Valdez runs aground and dumps ten million gallons of oil into the sea (1989)
- The Gulf War begins (1990)
- Sony Walkman debuts (1979)
- The murder trial of O.J. Simpson begins (1995)

Pair Shapes

DESCRIPTION: Pairs will make letters or shapes with their bodies.

SUPPLIES: CD or cassette player, lively music

Have participants form pairs. In each pair, have one person be in group one and the other person be in group two. Group one must form a circle going clockwise, and group two forms a circle around group one, going counterclockwise. Play some lively music, and instruct each group to walk in a circle in its assigned direction.

After a few moments, stop the music and call out a letter or shape. Players must find their partners and work together to use their bodies to make that letter or shape. For example, if you call out the letter O, each person must make up part of the letter O, combining with his or her partner to make up the whole letter. (One person can't do the whole shape or letter with the other partner just watching, nor can each person make up the whole shape or letter, resulting in two shapes or letters. Partners need to work together quickly to make the shape or letter together.)

The last pair to form the correct shape or letter is out of the game. Continue stopping and starting the music and calling out shapes or letters until only one pair is left.

Pillow Polo

DESCRIPTION: Players will try to score goals using pillows and a Ping-Pong ball.

SUPPLIES: masking tape, pillow for each player, Ping-Pong ball

Use masking tape to mark two goals, one at each end of the playing area. Then find the center of the field and mark the spot with an X.

Have players form two teams of five or more. Each team should designate a forward and a goalie. Forwards should stand at the X in the center of the field, and goalies should stand in front of the other team's goal line. Remaining players may be positioned anywhere on the field.

Give each person a pillow and

SAY:
Use the pillow to roll the Ping-Pong ball along the floor. You may touch the ball only with your pillow. Score points by moving the ball across your goal line.

Drop the ball over the X and let the game begin.

Starting Lineup

DESCRIPTION: Participants will work together to line up in order of age while blindfolded.

SUPPLIES: blindfolds

Explain to participants that they're going to play a game that forces them to be vulnerable. Have each person put on a blindfold.

SAY:
Not only will you have to be vulnerable by blindfolding yourself, but you'll also have to reveal your age. The goal of this game is to form a straight line in order of age while blindfolded. Oh yeah, in addition to being blindfolded, you also may not talk! Figure out a way

After players line up in a straight line, have participants take off their blindfolds. Have them double-check to make sure they're in a straight line and in order of age.

Stick 'Em

DESCRIPTION: Players will try to stick masking tape strips on one another while keeping tape strips off themselves.

SUPPLIES: masking tape

Have everyone gather in the center of the playing area. Give everyone three strips of masking tape, each about two to three inches in length.

Establish boundaries for the game, and explain that participants will have two minutes to place their masking tape strips on other players, while at the same time preventing anyone else from placing masking tape on them.

Tape may be placed only on the arms, legs, and back of a person; anywhere else is considered off limits. Tape may not be placed on anyone's bare skin; only on clothing. Also, each tape piece must be placed on a different person.

Any tape acquired during play must also be removed and placed on others. Therefore, although a person may quickly get rid of his or her original tape, there's a good chance more pieces will be picked up along the way.

Emphasize the importance of safety by asking that participants look out for one another.

Play the game, calling time after two minutes.

See how many people are left with no tape in hand or on themselves. Ask these players to sit while everyone else plays a second round. This time, allow only one minute for play. Again, call time and see if any more people have earned the right to sit.

Continue with rounds lasting fifteen seconds. Each of these rounds will have as a winner the person with the least number of tape pieces in hand and on his or her body. Play until only one person is left.

Triple Softball

DESCRIPTION: Participants will play softball with a twist—three teams instead of two!

SUPPLIES: softball, bats, gloves

Everyone knows how to play softball with two teams, but why not try playing with three teams? Make sure teams each have an equal number of players—at least five. All of the normal rules of softball apply.

The game starts with Team 1 at bat and Teams 2 and 3 out in the field. After Team 1 has three outs, Team 2 is at bat, and Teams 1 and 3 play the field. After Team 2 has three outs, Team 3 is at bat, and Teams 1 and 2 play the field, and so on. Keep score or play just for fun!

Zany Mini-Golf

DESCRIPTION: Participants will play a silly and unique version of miniature golf.

SUPPLIES: Ping-Pong balls, tees, paper cups, nails, brooms, mop handles, and prizes (such as pieces of candy)

Lay out a course of three to nine golf "holes" in the churchyard using obstacles such as bricks, boxes, trees, and old tires between the tees and holes. Use paper cups as the holes by laying them on their sides and nailing them to the ground. Have participants use brooms or mop handles as putters and Ping-Pong balls as golf balls. If families are participating, have members of each family compete together by taking turns putting as a team.

Game Leader TIP

MAKE THIS GAME EVEN MORE ZANY BY AWARDING SILLY AND CREATIVE PRIZES AT DIFFERENT HOLES. FOR EXAMPLE, ONE PRIZE COULD BE AWARDED FOR THE MOST STROKES ON A PARTICULAR HOLE. ANOTHER PRIZE COULD BE AWARDED TO THOSE WHO MAKE A PUTT WITH THEIR EYES CLOSED.

SECTION 2

Low-Key
GAMES

ABC Conversation

DESCRIPTION: Participants will create an impromptu conversation by starting each phrase with the next letter in the alphabet.

SUPPLIES: none

Have participants form a circle.

SAY:

You're going to create a conversation beginning with one person and going in a circle. Each person needs to say only one sentence, and the next person has to say a sentence that makes sense as a response. The trick is that the first sentence or phrase has to start with A, the next with B, and so on.

Here's an example of an ABC conversation:

Person one: "Another day at church."

Person two: "Believe it or not, I haven't been here for two months."

Person three: "Can I believe it!? I've been so busy too."

The conversation continues until the circle reaches Z or someone can't think of anything to say. If that happens, the person is out of the game and the next person in the circle should pick up the conversation where it left off.

Biblical Family Feud

DESCRIPTION: Participants will have a good time choosing the most popular answers in particular Bible categories.

SUPPLIES: paper, pen or pencil

Before the game, survey a group of people in your church for their answers in the following categories. Record their responses.

- Name one of the fruits of the Spirit.
- Name a spiritual gift.

- Name one of Jesus' disciples.
- Name one of Joseph's sons.
- Name a book in the Old Testament.
- Name a book in the New Testament.
- Name one of the Ten Commandments.
- Name one of the plagues on Egypt.
- Name a person in Jesus' lineage.
- Name a parable of Jesus.

After you have surveyed several people, compile the results. Rank the results from the most common response to the least common response in each category. Limit the rankings to no more than ten responses in each category.

Have participants form two teams. Each team should select one person to represent the team at the beginning of the first round. Explain that these two players need to come up with what they believe was the most popular response in the category you name.

Name a category from your survey, and let the two representatives guess. The person who comes up with the response highest on your list has the option to have his or her team continue guessing the category or pass to the other team.

If a team chooses to guess the rest of the responses, they must come up with all the remaining responses in that category without making a mistake. If they make a mistake, they forfeit the category to the other team. If the other team makes a mistake, the play switches back to the first team. Keep going on the category until all the answers are revealed. The team that gives the final response gets credit for that category.

For the next round, have teams choose new representatives. Continue playing until all the categories have been played.

Board Game Tournament

DESCRIPTION: Participants will play board games "round-robin" style.

SUPPLIES: one board game for every four people, tables, chairs

Set up the tables in a circle or square with chairs on both the inside and the outside of the configuration. Have everyone take a seat. Place board games on the tables so two people inside the circle and two people outside can play against each other. If you have a large group, you may need more than one circle or square of tables.

Explain that players will play the board game in front of them until you call time after ten minutes. At that time, everyone should shift one position to his or her right, leaving the board game in the same spot. Then players should continue playing the games, with two new people taking over for the two that just left.

Continue for about an hour, switching every ten minutes.

Game Leader TIP

THIS TOURNAMENT WORKS BEST IF YOU USE GAMES THAT EVERYONE IS FAMILIAR WITH, SUCH AS YAHTZEE, CHECKERS, MONOPOLY, JENGA, DOMINOES, AND SO ON.

Game Leader TIP

IT'S A GOOD IDEA TO TAKE SOME TIME TO TALK ABOUT THE DIFFERENT GAMES AT THE BEGINNING SO EVERYONE KNOWS THE RULES.

Bringing Up Baby

DESCRIPTION: Participants will work in teams to properly nurture their "babies."

SUPPLIES: four each: baby dolls, baby bathtubs or basins, bottles of shampoo, towels, cloth diapers, tubes of ointment, containers of baby powder, doll outfits; eight diaper pins; water

Have players form four teams. Give each group a baby doll, a baby bathtub or basin full of water, shampoo, a towel, a cloth diaper, ointment, baby powder, two diaper pins, and a doll outfit. Tell everyone that in this game, each person is allowed to use only one hand: the hand he or she doesn't normally write with. Teammates must decide how to work together to care for their "baby."

Teams must accomplish these tasks in order: bathe the baby and shampoo its hair without letting it drown; dry the baby, remembering to support its head; rub ointment on the baby's bottom and powder it; pin a diaper on the baby; and dress the baby.

The team that completes this challenge the fastest is the winning team.

Calendar Corrections

DESCRIPTION: Team members will work together to identify mistakes on a calendar.

SUPPLIES: photocopies of calendars, markers

Before the game, prepare a yearly calendar with various holidays and important events listed. However, make a few changes in each month. For example, switch the date of Christmas, place the Fourth of July on the fifth, delete one Monday and include a second Sunday, include thirty-two days in January, change birthdays and holidays. Use your creativity to come up with some obvious and some difficult changes to identify. Make a copy of the calendar for each team.

Have participants form groups of five to eight people. Give each team a marker. Allow five minutes for each team to identify as many of the inaccuracies as possible.

Choose Your Own Ending

DESCRIPTION: Participants will write stories without endings, then finish each other's stories.

SUPPLIES: paper, pens or pencils, any three objects that can be easily displayed (such as a sculpture, a kitchen utensil, and a roll of toilet paper)

Before the game, set out your three objects where everyone will be able to see them.

Give each person paper and a pen or pencil. Direct everyone's attention to the three objects on display.

When the stories are done, have participants read their stories aloud to the group.

Dressing Derby

DESCRIPTION: Players will race to see who can get dressed the fastest.

SUPPLIES: an equal number of silly clothing items for each team (such as a hat, a large dress or pair of pants, pantyhose, a jacket, a scarf, gloves, and sunglasses)

Have participants form equal teams. Give each team a set of silly clothing.

When the game begins, one person on each team puts on all the clothing over his or her own clothes. Once that person has completely dressed in all the items, he or she should remove them quickly and give them to a teammate, who will repeat this same procedure and give them to a third person.

Players continue dressing and undressing until everyone on the team has dressed and undressed. The first team to complete the sequence wins.

Fill in the Blanks

DESCRIPTION: Participants will work in pairs to fill in the blanks and create funny stories.

SUPPLIES: photocopies of the "My Amazing Day" handout (p. 39), pens or pencils

Before the game, make one photocopy of the "My Amazing Day" handout (p. 39) for every two people.

Have participants form pairs.

Game Leader TIP

IF PARTICIPANTS WOULD LIKE TO PLAY THIS GAME AGAIN, GIVE EACH PAIR A SHEET OF PAPER AND A PEN OR PENCIL AND HAVE PARTNERS CREATE A NEW STORY WITH MISSING WORDS, USING THE HANDOUT AS A MODEL. WHEN THEY'RE FINISHED, HAVE PAIRS EXCHANGE STORIES WITH EACH OTHER AND FILL IN THE BLANKS.

SAY:

In this game, you'll need to work together with your partner to create a funny story. Here's how it works: In a moment, I'll give one person in each pair a story with several words left out. That person will need to ask the other person to give him or her some words to fill in the blanks. Each blank has a type of word listed under it. For example, if you see a blank that says "plural noun," your partner might say something like "trees."

Give one partner in each pair a copy of the "My Amazing Day" handout and a pen or pencil.

SAY:

Be sure your partner doesn't see the handout until the story is finished. Ask your partner to help you fill in the blanks to create a story. When you're finished with your story, I'll ask you to share it with the group.

Give pairs a few minutes to finish their stories and then have each pair share its story.

My Amazing Day

Today I got up at _____ o'clock. I put on my
(number)

favorite _____ _____. I ate
(a color)   (an article of clothing)

_____ and _____ for breakfast.
(plural noun)   (plural noun)

Before I left my house, I watched a little _____ on TV.
(TV show)

On my way to _____, I ran into _____.
(place)   (name of a celebrity or another famous person)

We _____ for a while, and then we decided to go to
(-ed verb)

_____. At the restaurant, I ordered _____
(name of a restaurant)   (plural noun)

and my companion ordered _____. When we were
(noun)

finished, we decided to fly to _____ and_____.
(an exotic locale)   (a fun pastime)

When we were there, we saw _____ and _____.
(a famous foreign landmark)   (another famous landmark)

Then we decided it was time to go home. I couldn't believe how much

the plane tickets cost— _____! When we got back to
(an amount of money)

the airport, I went home in my _____. I went to my
(type of car)

_____ and called my friend _____ on
(noun)   (name of a cartoon character)

the telephone. My friend was _____ when I told him
(adjective)

(or her) about my incredible day.

Food Fight

DESCRIPTION: Teams will catapult pieces of cereal into large bowls in a limited amount of time.

SUPPLIES: masking tape, cereal, a large bowl for each team, a plastic spoon for each participant

Before the game, use masking tape to mark a line on the floor.

Have participants form teams of four or five, and direct teams to sit in clusters behind the line you marked beforehand (which they cannot cross). Place large bowls five feet beyond the line, one in front of each team.

Distribute plastic spoons and a generous amount of cereal to each group.

SAY:
When I give the signal, use your spoons to shoot cereal into your team's bowl. At the end of three minutes, the team with the most cereal in its bowl will win.

Get Off My Back

DESCRIPTION: Players must guess the secret items listed on their backs.

SUPPLIES: self-stick notes, pens or pencils

Give each player a stack of ten self-stick notes, and have players form pairs. Explain that when you name a category, players will think of an example within that category and write the example on a self-stick note. Players should be careful not to let their partners or anyone else see their answers. Call out the following categories.

- **a Bible character**

- **a TV character**
- **a cartoon**
- **a song**
- **a profession**
- **a restaurant**
- **a specific product found in a grocery store**
- **a book title**
- **a specific product found at a convenience store**
- **a video game**

Then ask each player to stick the answers on his or her partner's back. When you say "go," each person should find someone else and begin asking that person questions about the answers on his or her back, specifying the category. Players may ask only yes-or-no questions. When a person guesses the right answer on a self-stick note, his or her partner will remove that note and give it to the guesser who will write down the number of questions it took to get to the answer. Then he or she must move on and ask questions of another person. Players cannot use the same person twice in a row. If your group is large enough, establish a rule that they may not use the same player twice at all.

After several minutes, stop the game and have players total the number of points written on their self-stick notes. Add five points for each note still stuck to the back. The person with the lowest number is the winner.

Looking for...

DESCRIPTION: Players will follow instructions to form groups in a fast-paced manner.

SUPPLIES: none

Explain to participants that you'll call out categories, and in twenty seconds or less they must join with others who fit the same descriptions they do. Anyone who doesn't join with at least one other person in the same category at the end of the twenty seconds is eliminated from the game. To begin, have the whole group walk around, chanting "looking for..." repeatedly until you shout out a category. Call time after twenty seconds, and eliminate anyone who didn't find a partner or a group in time. Then begin the game again. Continue play until just one or two people are left. Use the following categories, or make up your own.

- **same hair color**
- **same birthday month**
- **same color shirt**
- **same color pants**
- **same shoe type**
- **same color socks**
- **same age**
- **same favorite food**
- **same favorite drink**

Make Me a New Face

DESCRIPTION: Participants will draw faces on a paper bag—which is on someone else's head.

SUPPLIES: paper bags, markers

Have participants form groups of four. Give each group one paper bag and assorted markers. Instruct one team member in each group to place the paper bag over his or her head and keep it there during the game. With markers handy, players will take turns answering questions by adding facial features to their group member. Each player must add only one facial feature at a time, then pass the marker to the next player.

Questions will allow teams to complete a face after six questions, if each team associates the correct facial feature with each question. The first team to complete a face wins. A finished face includes eyes, ears, nose, mouth, eyebrows, and eyelashes.

Ask these questions:

- **What can open or shut when it doesn't want to participate?** (eyes, ears, mouth)
- **What can flutter and flow against the sun and wind?** (eyelids, eyelashes)
- **What can be plugged up?** (nose, mouth, ears)
- **What can show anger or surprise?** (eyebrows, mouth)
- **What can detect whether food is palatable?** (nose, mouth)
- **What can appreciate the waves rolling in or the wind in the trees?** (ears, eyes)
- **What can show others how you're feeling?** (eyes, mouth)
- **What can open wide and take in countless delights?** (mouth, nose, eyes, ears)

Mini-Me Racers

DESCRIPTION: Players will "race" mini versions of themselves by blowing them across the floor.

SUPPLIES: photocopies of "Racer Outline" on page 44, pennies, transparent tape, card-stock paper, pencils, crayons, markers, masking tape

Before the game, photocopy the "Racer Outline" on page 44 on card-stock paper. You'll need one copy on card stock for each person. Place a strip of masking tape on the floor and write "finish line" on the tape. Place a second strip of tape about three feet from the first and write "start" on it.

Give each person a copy of the "Racer Outline" and a penny. Make pencils, markers, and crayons available. Tell players to cut out their racers and draw themselves on the front. Be sure they know this isn't an art contest—how well they draw has nothing to do with whether they win or lose.

fold
here

attach
coin
here

Have players fold their racers on the dotted line and use transparent tape to attach a penny to the bottom flap, as shown in the illustration at left.

Have players set their racers behind the starting line you marked beforehand. When you say "go," players should attempt to blow their racers across the finish line. If they blow too hard, the pieces will fall over. If they aim their streams of air correctly, the racers will scoot across the floor. If a racer falls, its owner must start again from the starting line.

RACER OUTLINE

Partner Scramble

DESCRIPTION: Players will race to find their partners and accomplish various tasks.

SUPPLIES: none

Have participants form two equal groups, and label the groups A and B. Have all the A's form a circle facing out. Have all the B's form a circle around circle A, facing in. Everyone should be facing another person. This person will be his or her partner for the game.

Instruct circle A to rotate clockwise and circle B to rotate counterclockwise until you shout out a task.

SAY:

When I shout out a task, you must stop rotating, find your partner, and accomplish the task. The last pair to do so will be eliminated from the game.

Shout out tasks, eliminating one pair each round, until just one pair is left.

Call out the following tasks, or make up your own.

- **Find your partner and stand back to back.**
- **Find your partner and exchange a high five.**
- **Find your partner and exchange a funny face.**
- **Find your partner and touch his or her nose.**
- **Find your partner and pat his or her head three times.**
- **Find your partner and scratch his or her back.**
- **Find your partner and touch his or her big toe.**
- **Find your partner and remove his or her right shoe.**
- **Find your partner and count his or her teeth fillings**.

Person, Place, or Thing

DESCRIPTION: Participants will create brain teasers about people, places, or things.

SUPPLIES: pens or pencils, paper

Have participants form groups of five or six people. Distribute pencils and paper. Instruct each person to write a brain teaser about a person, place, or thing. The objective is to give accurate details but disguise them in clever rhymes or riddles.

The only rule is this: If the brain teaser is about a person, the brain teaser must include information on a place and a thing associated with that person. If it's a place, the brain teaser must include a person and a thing associated with that place. If it's a thing, the brain teaser must include a person and a place associated with the thing.

Next, each group will select two brain teasers to use in competition. Each group will read its two brain teasers, identifying the answer as a person, place, or thing. The group that correctly identifies the answer is awarded a point. If no one guesses correctly and the brain teaser meets the requirements of the game, the group who stumped the others gets a point.

The team with the most points wins.

Pin the Prize

DESCRIPTION: Blindfolded players will tape their names on the wall to see who gets nearest the prize.

SUPPLIES: prize (such as a dollar bill or a candy bar), small pieces of paper, pens or pencils, masking tape, blindfold

Before the game, tape a prize, such as a dollar bill or a candy bar, on a blank wall.

Give each person a small piece of paper, a pen or pencil, and a piece of tape. Have each person write his or her name on the piece of paper.

Have players take turns putting on a blindfold and taping their names on the wall. Whoever "pins" his or her name nearest the prize wins it. Players must keep one hand behind their backs while taping their names on the wall. They aren't allowed to feel around on the wall.

Pressure Pass

DESCRIPTION: People will pass objects around a circle in as many different ways as possible.

SUPPLIES: none

Have participants form a circle. Ask each person to contribute an object that could easily be passed around the circle, such as a ring, a bracelet, a comb, a photo, lipstick, or a key. It doesn't matter if objects are similar in type, only that each may be passed easily from person to person.

One person starts by passing his or her object to the right in an unusual way. For example, a comb might be balanced on the nose before being passed by hand to the next person, or a photo might be passed around the neck three times before moving on.

Players should pass the object around the circle, with each person passing it the way its owner did. When the object gets back to its owner, talk briefly about how easy it was to pass one object around the circle.

Tell participants that now, whenever you yell "go," the person to the immediate right of the last person to start an object must start passing his or her object in a creative way. It's a good idea to wait until an object has passed three or four people before starting another. Explain that players should try to pass their objects in different and creative ways.

In no time, many objects will be passed around the circle, all ending with their starting players.

Play one more time, but add the rule that once an object is "in play" (being passed around circle), it must continue throughout the game. Keep adding objects until everyone in the circle has added his or her object. See how long players can pass all the objects around the circle.

Progressive Story

DESCRIPTION: Players will work together to complete a story based on an unfinished drawing.

SUPPLIES: newsprint or dry erase board, marker

Have participants form teams of three. Explain that all the teams will leave the meeting room while you draw something on the board. One team at a time, teams will be ushered back into the room and given three minutes to draw the next scene in the story. After each team has contributed to the story with its own scene, that team must immediately leave the meeting room again. No team is allowed to see other teams at work.

Instruct all the teams to leave the room, then draw a simple version of a scene on newsprint or a dry erase board. Be sure to leave plenty of room for teams to draw. Try one of these scenes or your own idea.

- a person letting go of a bunch of balloons
- an elderly man bending down to pick up a hundred dollar bill
- a baby crawling toward a plate full of cookies
- a choir singing in front of a swimming pool
- a couple of children climbing a fence

When you're finished drawing, call in one team. Have that team quickly draw the next scene in the story, then leave the room. Call in the next team to draw the next scene, and so on.

When all the teams have drawn a scene, usher everyone back into the room. Have teams tell the story in sequence, with each team describing a scene another team drew.

Then ask teams to retell the story, this time describing the scenes they drew.

Signal Swap

DESCRIPTION: In this rhythm game, players must exchange signals in a fast-paced manner.

SUPPLIES: chairs

Have participants sit in a circle. If you have more than ten people, form more than one circle. Explain that everyone must come up with an original signal—either a face or hand gesture, or combination of both—to identify himself or herself. For example, one person's signal may be a specific funny face, while another person's signal may be placing his hands on top of his head. The more creative the signals, the better. After everyone has thought of a signal, go around the circle and have everyone demonstrate his or her signal to the rest of the group. Instruct the group to try to remember as many signals as possible.

SAY:
This game is played like Rhythm, but instead of using numbers, we're using signals. The rhythm pattern is slapping your hands on your thighs twice, clapping your hands twice, and snapping your fingers twice. We'll all do the rhythm pattern together.

Someone in the circle will replace the snapping with signals, first that person's own signal and then someone else's. Then that other person will take a turn, also filling in with his or her signal and then someone else's at the appropriate time during the rhythm pattern. This pattern will be repeated over and over until someone disrupts the rhythm. That person will then be eliminated from the circle. The game continues in this way until just one person is left.

Do a practice round once, and then begin the game. Be sure to begin the rhythm pattern at a very slow pace, speeding it up as the game progresses. Eliminate anyone who reverses the order of signals, pauses too long, gives a signal that doesn't exist, or otherwise disrupts the rhythm of the game. If time allows, play several rounds and have everyone change signals each time.

Toe Tap

DESCRIPTION: Partners will compete to try to tap each other's toes first.

SUPPLIES: none

Have players choose a partner. Explain that players must try to tap their partners' feet with their toes without letting their partners tap theirs. But pairs must play with their hands joined together and their arms stretched up in the air to form a "bridge." The first person in the pair to tap his or her partner's toes three times wins.

Have all the pairs play simultaneously. After all the winners are determined, have the losers sit out and the winners form new pairs. Continue eliminating the losing partners until just one winner remains.

Tool Time

DESCRIPTION: Participants will try to quickly identify common kitchen objects and tools.

SUPPLIES: table, assortment of boxes, several kitchen objects (spatula, ladle, measuring cups, and so on), several tools (wrenches, drills, and so on), stopwatch, paper, pen or pencil

Before the game, set up a table with boxes on top. Place one of the kitchen objects or tools of your choice under each box.

Have all the players except one leave the room. Invite that person to lift the boxes one by one, identifying the objects by name. Keep track of how many objects the person identifies and how long he or she takes.

Allow the first player to stay in the room, and bring in another person. Let that person take a turn identifying objects, and keep track of how many objects the person identifies and the amount of time he or she takes. Continue until everyone has had a turn.

At the end of the game, see who correctly identified the most objects in the least amount of time.

Towers of Babel

DESCRIPTION: Teams will work together to see who can build the highest tower.

SUPPLIES: paper clips

Have participants form teams of five to ten. Give each team a box or two of paper clips.

Allow five to seven minutes for each team to build a tower of paper clips. The clips may be bent in various shapes, stacked, or clipped together. But all towers must be able to stand alone without assistance.

When time is up, see which team has been able to build the tallest tower.

Value Debate

DESCRIPTION: Participants will decide what's most important in life.

SUPPLIES: photocopies of the "Value Sheet" handout (p. 53), pens or pencils

Give each participant a copy of the "Value Sheet" handout and a pen or pencil. Have players fill out their handouts, placing the appropriate values in a column on the right side of the paper.

After everyone has answered, hold an auction. Award each item to the person who assigned it the most money on the handout.

If you play it with families, this game helps parents and their children see what their family members value.

When I Was a Kid

DESCRIPTION: Participants will try to guess which events happened to whom.

SUPPLIES: none

Have participants form two teams. Tell teams that each person should come up with a memorable story from his or her childhood days. The events can be funny, embarrassing, serious, or outlandish.

Give teams several minutes to meet and tell their stories. Teams should meet away from each other, in separate rooms if possible. Each team should choose which stories to share with the whole group—as many as time allows.

Each team should decide who will relate which stories. The person relating the story can be the one who actually experienced it or someone who tries to convince the other team the incident happened to him or her.

Game Leader TIP

IF YOU'RE PLAYING THIS GAME IN AN INTERGEN-ERATIONAL SETTING, IT'S FUN TO PUT KIDS ON ONE TEAM AND ADULTS ON THE OTHER.

Call teams together, and have them take turns telling stories. After someone tells a story, the other team should try to guess who really experienced the incident. Teams get one point for every correct guess, and one point for every time the other team guesses wrong.

Be sure both teams are allowed to relate the same number of incidents. The team with the most points at the end wins.

Value Sheet

Imagine that you have $50,000 to spend on the items listed below. You can invest all your money in one category or divide it between the items, placing more money on the items you value most and little or no money on the items you value least.

VALUE   AMOUNT I'D INVEST

1. to stop all disease $ _____

2. to stop world hunger $ _____

3. to make an investment that would guarantee a college education for my children $ _____

4. to find the real meaning of life $ _____

5. to be the most popular person in the world $ _____

6. to be a great world leader $ _____

7. to bring peace to all nations and destroy all weapons $ _____

8. to understand the entire Bible $ _____

9. to know the future $ _____

10. to travel anywhere in the world $ _____

11. to spend time with a special person $ _____

12. to buy all the things I ever wanted $ _____

Get-to-Know-You
GAMES

Bite the Lemon

DESCRIPTION: Participants will get to know each other by answering questions from other members of the group.

SUPPLIES: several lemons, peeled but whole

Have everyone sit in a circle. Begin passing a lemon around the circle like a "hot potato." After a short while, yell "stop!" The person who last touched the lemon must hold on to the lemon. The person who passed the lemon to the last person then may ask the person holding the lemon any question on any subject. The person with the lemon can choose either to answer the question or to bite the lemon without answering the question.

After the person has answered the question or bit the lemon, the group begins passing the lemon again. If the person chose to bite the lemon, be sure to replace it with a new one.

Game Leader TIP

IT'S GREAT TO HAVE A CAMERA ON HAND TO CATCH THE FACIAL EXPRESSIONS OF THOSE WHO CHOOSE TO BITE THE LEMON.

Chat Circles

DESCRIPTION: Participants will pair up when the music stops and discover information about each other.

SUPPLIES: lively music, cassette or CD player

Have players form two groups, group A and group B. Have all the A's form a circle facing out (circle A), and all the B's form a circle around circle A, facing in (circle B). Instruct circle A to rotate clockwise, and circle B to rotate counterclockwise.

> ## SAY:
> We'll use these circles to help us get to know each other better. I'll be playing music, and when the music stops you should stop rotating so everyone in circle A is facing someone in circle B. After you stop, I'll call out a question you'll then discuss with the person you're facing.

Ask these questions one at a time when you stop the music, or come up with questions of your own.

- **What's your middle name?**
- **Where do you go to school or work?**
- **What's your favorite color and why?**
- **What's your favorite TV show?**
- **What's one talent or hobby you have?**
- **What's your shoe size?**
- **How many siblings do you have?**
- **What's your birth date?**
- **What makes you laugh?**

Colors, Candy, Careers

DESCRIPTION: This game tests the memory and helps players learn more about each other.

SUPPLIES: stopwatch

This game is played in three rounds—the faster the better. Have the players form a circle. Ask one player to say the name of his or her favorite color. The next player in the circle must repeat what player one said and then add his or her own favorite color. Player three then repeats the answers of players one and two, then adds his or her own. This continues until the entire circle names all their favorite colors. The first player must repeat the colors from the whole circle.

> **Game Leader TIP**
>
> DON'T ALLOW TALKATIVE PARTICIPANTS TO EXPAND ON THE REASONS THEY LIKE THE COLOR BLUE OR WHY M&M'S ARE THEIR FAVORITE CANDY. ANSWERS SHOULD BE LIMITED TO ONE WORD.

Immediately launch into round two, which consists of stating the names of players' favorite candies. Finally, play the third round—each person should announce his or her career or a career he or she would like to have someday.

Repeat the game, timing the group to see how quickly they can complete each round.

Dark Discussions

DESCRIPTION: Players will form groups while blindfolded and discover new information about each other.

SUPPLIES: blindfolds

This game is best played in an open area outside or in a large room free of hazards.

Everyone should be blindfolded and must carefully walk around until they touch someone else. If necessary, position yourself and other volunteers around the area to keep players from wandering too far from the group.

When two people have found each other, those two must stay

connected while each person "finds" someone else to connect with so the group totals four. Once four people have connected, all four group members must remove their blindfolds and find out one new thing about each person in their group. For example, a player might discover someone's name, or find out what that person ate for dinner the day before.

Encourage play to continue simultaneously, so that some groups will be discussing while other people are walking around still blindfolded. When group members have finished discovering information about each other, players must replace their blindfolds and continue playing. Emphasize that whenever players connect with people they previously connected with, they must find out *new* information.

If a blindfolded person accidentally bumps into an already connected group, that group should tell the blindfolded person and send him or her on. Continue playing until all group members have been mixed up very well.

Dessert Shuffle

DESCRIPTION: Participants will try to guess what desserts they are while meeting others in the group.

SUPPLIES: self-stick notes, a pen or pencil

Before the game, write the names of various desserts on self-stick notes, with a different dessert on each note. You'll need one dessert-labeled self-stick note for each person.

Have participants stand in a line, shoulder-to-shoulder with their backs to you. Place a dessert-labeled self-stick note on each person's back. When you've labeled everyone with a dessert tag, have players turn around and face you.

SAY:

I'd like you to spend the next few minutes milling around and trying to determine what type of dessert you are. You may ask yes or no questions only, and you may not tell anyone what type of dessert he or she is—you can only answer that person's questions. If you've asked enough questions and you think you know what type of dessert you are, you can ask someone by saying, "Am I a _____?"

Give people several minutes to guess what desserts they are. When all the players have determined what desserts they are, congratulate everyone's accomplishment.

Famous Authors

DESCRIPTION: Participants will make up book titles that describe their lives and try to match the titles with the correct participants.

SUPPLIES: paper, pens or pencils, access to a photocopy machine

Give each person paper and a pen or pencil, and instruct each person to write down his or her name and a make-believe book title that describes his or her life.

Have a volunteer collect the cards and quickly copy all the titles on one piece of paper, then make enough photocopies for every participant.

Hand out the papers with the titles on them.

SAY:
These are the titles of all the books. Let's try to match the titles with the people who wrote them. Walk around and ask people questions about their lives in order to find matches. You can't ask anyone directly what his or her title is. You can ask questions only regarding the person's life and make a guess as to what the title may be.

After several minutes, identify the correct author for each title and find out who guessed the most correct titles.

Foot Skits

DESCRIPTION: Partners will use their feet to introduce each other.

SUPPLIES: several markers, scraps of material (optional), transparent tape (optional), two chairs, sheet

Have participants form pairs with people they don't know. Give participants a few minutes to get to know each other, then have everyone gather in the center of the room.

SAY:

I'd like you to introduce your partner, but I don't want you to introduce that person in the traditional way. I'd like each of you to take off one of your shoes, draw a face on your foot, and have your foot introduce your partner's foot.

Distribute markers, and give pairs a few minutes to draw their faces and think about what they're going to say about each other. Encourage participants to create personalities for their feet. You might even want to provide scraps of material and tape so they can dress up their feet. As pairs are working, line up two chairs at the front of your meeting area, facing each other. Place a sheet over the chairs to serve as a curtain. Instruct pairs to come up, one pair at a time, and lie on their backs on the ground behind the chairs. Players should place their feet on top of the curtain and introduce each other with their feet.

When everyone is finished, congratulate players for their bravery and creativity!

I Believe in Music

DESCRIPTION: Groups will get to know each other by sharing meaningful song lyrics.

SUPPLIES: paper, markers

Have participants form two teams. Distribute paper and markers, and instruct each person to write down a line from a song that best describes his or her personality. The song shouldn't necessarily be the person's current favorite tune, but a single line that describes who that person is.

Collect the papers and place them in two piles—one for each team.

Tell players you'll be reading the song lines from each team aloud to the other team. The other team will have five seconds to come up with the title of the song that the line is from.

If the guessing team guesses correctly, that team gets two hundred points. If they guess incorrectly, the opposing team scores one hundred points. As a three hundred–point follow-up question, give the guessing team ten seconds to discuss and guess who wrote down that song line. Award the points to the opposing team if they guess incorrectly.

Game Leader TIP

AFTER YOU READ A SONG LINE AND THE OTHER TEAM HAS HAD A CHANCE TO GUESS WHAT THE SONG IS AND WHO CHOSE IT, YOU MAY WANT TO ASK THE PLAYER WHO CHOSE IT TO EXPLAIN WHY THAT LINE REPRESENTS HIM OR HER.

If You...

DESCRIPTION: Players will find common interests by switching places in a circle of chairs.

SUPPLIES: chairs

Have players sit in a circle. You should have one less chair than you have players. The player without a chair must stand in the middle of the circle. Explain that you're going to read a series of statements that all begin with the words "If you..." You'll then say "go." At the word "go," all those players who have done what the statement describes must find a new chair to sit in. In the meantime, the player in the middle of the circle should try to find a place to sit.

This is one of those games that has no real winners, so you can play for as long as you can come up with questions. Be sure to throw in a few "If you..." statements that you're positive describe everyone. That way, the entire circle must get up and move. Here are a few to get you started:

- **If you have ever fallen asleep in church...**
- **If you have ever been a shepherd in a Christmas play...**
- **If you scored an A on a test in the last week...**
- **If you have ever put off your weekend homework until Sunday night...**
- **If you have ever burned your dinner...**
- **If you have ever spilled something in a restaurant...**
- **If you have slipped and fallen in a public place...**
- **If you have put your shoes on the wrong feet...**
- **If you have eaten a peanut butter and mayonnaise sandwich...**
- **If you like pineapple on your pizza...**
- **If you know all the words to (name a current top-ten hit)...**
- **If you know Psalm 23 by heart...**
- **If you have a dog at home...**
- **If you have a driver's license...**
- **If you have ever dented a car...**
- **If you have ever belched while on a date...**
- **If you can remember your first-grade teacher's name...**
- **If you can remember your own name...**
- **If you talk to plants...**
- **If you can play Mozart on an instrument...**
- **If you have ever listened to Mozart...**
- **If you know who Mozart is...**

- **If you have ever dressed up as Santa...**
- **If you like Kermit better than any other Muppet...**
- **If you like Goofy better than Mickey Mouse...**
- **If you have ever slept past noon...**

Impersonation

DESCRIPTION: Participants will impersonate each other's actions while remembering each other's names.

SUPPLIES: none

Have players stand in a circle. Instruct one person in the circle to introduce himself or herself and tell about something he or she likes to do, while pantomiming that action. For example, one person may say, "My name is Holly, and I like to golf." While she talked, Holly would pantomime golfing.

The next person in the circle should then repeat what the first person said and pantomimed, then introduce himself or herself, including a new pantomimed action. For example, the second person may say, "This is Holly and she likes to golf" while pantomiming golfing; then "I'm Ed and I like to fish," while pretending to throw out a fishing line.

The third person in the circle should repeat the words and actions of the first two people and then add his or her own. Have players continue introducing themselves until they make it all the way around the circle.

In My Day

DESCRIPTION: Participants of different ages will take turns giving clues to items or terms commonly used in their generation.

SUPPLIES: index cards, pens or pencils

Have participants divide into two teams: everyone over twenty on one team, people under twenty on another team. Give each team a supply of index cards and pens or pencils.

Invite each group to write down clues pertaining to various items or terms commonly used in their generation. For example, adults might write, "This word was commonly used in the 1960s and 1970s; this word also sounds similar to what one would find on a vinyl record. Answer: groovy."

When teams have finished writing clues, give them an opportunity to quiz each other. If you like, keep score and see which generation is the most knowledgeable about the other.

If teams need help coming up with clues, give them these ideas: musical terms, slang terms, dress styles, cars, school subjects, dating terminology, and popular movies and books. Both adults and young people may be surprised to learn how much they actually have in common.

In Touch

DESCRIPTION: Participants will learn more about each other when they use their sense of touch.

SUPPLIES: none

This is a great icebreaker game, especially to begin an intergenerational meeting.

Invite everyone in the room to stand and mill about. No one should say anything, or ask a question, until you give an instruction. Each time you give an instruction, however, all players should follow your instruction by asking a question that will help them get better acquainted with someone else in the group.

As the group is milling around the room, call out these instructions one at a time:

- **Tap someone on the shoulder and ask his or her name.**

- **Shake someone's hand and ask about his or her favorite food.**

- **Give someone a hug and ask about his or her favorite song.**

- **Rub someone's shoulders and ask about the person's hobbies.**

- **Link arms with someone and ask about all the places he or she has lived.**

- **High five someone's hand and ask the person to describe a favorite relative.**
- **Patty-cake someone's hands and ask about the most outrageous thing the person has ever done.**
- **Pat someone's head and ask about a goal that person has for his or her life.**

Likes/Dislikes

DESCRIPTION: Participants will interact with others in the group, trying to find matches for the specific likes or dislikes they've drawn from a basket.

SUPPLIES: slips of paper, pens or pencils, hat or basket

Give each participant two slips of paper and a pen or pencil. Ask players to each write something they really like on one slip, and a strong dislike on the other. The first slip should read, "I like _____." The second slip should read, "I don't like _____." Collect the slips of paper in a basket or hat.

Next ask each player to draw two slips of paper and search to find the people the slips belong to. Give participants lots of time to interact and make matches while learning about others in the group.

Lock 'n' Guess

DESCRIPTION: Players will try to guess the features of partners who are locked back-to-back with them.

SUPPLIES: whistle

Have participants spread out throughout the room. Explain that players should start moving quickly around the room, without running.

When you blow a whistle, each person should find a partner he or she doesn't know very well. If you're playing this game in an intergenerational setting, require people to pair up with players from other generations, but not with people from their families.

After pairing up, partners must each share the following three pieces of information about themselves: full name (including middle name); favorite sport, hobby, or craft; and the animal that best reflects his or her personality and why. Add that players should try to remember as much information about each other as possible.

Once both partners have exchanged information, they must stand back-to-back, arms locked. When everyone is locked back-to-back, call out a body feature which may or may not be easily recognized. Features may include hair color, hair length, shirt style, shoe brand, whether the person is wearing a belt, pant length (touching floor or not), and so on.

While locked back-to-back, partners should try to correctly guess the feature called without looking at the person. After they guess each feature, ask partners to turn, face each other, and see if their guesses were correct.

If both people are correct, they yell and share a high five. If one person is wrong, this player must run five times around the partner who guessed correctly, who should stand still. If both people are wrong, they must join hands, then run and gently scratch the backs of any five people in the room.

When the first round is complete, instruct players to begin moving around the room again. Whenever you sound the whistle, everyone must quickly find a new partner. Information is exchanged, arms are locked back-to-back, and the game continues as before.

Play at least five rounds, then see who can recall the most information about their partners.

Name Scramble

DESCRIPTION: Participants will learn each other's names through a rhythm game.

SUPPLIES: two wood blocks or books for each person

Give each participant two wood blocks or books, and have everyone sit in a circle. Appoint one person to be the leader. Begin by having everyone bang their wood blocks or books on the floor. Then have everyone bang their blocks or books together. Practice this a few times until you've got a rhythm going. Next, explain to participants that on the first bang, one person will say his or her own name, and on the second bang, the name of another person in the group. That person will then follow the rhythm to say his or her own name, followed by the name of another person in the group. Players should continue this rhythm and calling out names until someone makes a mistake.

When someone makes a mistake, the leader yells, "Scramble!" At that time, participants should get up and find out the names of three people they don't know. Then they should exchange their pieces of wood or books with the last person they talk to and find a new place to sit.

Repeat the game until you've played it several times and players have met each other.

Personality Pictionary

DESCRIPTION: Participants will take turns drawing and guessing the identities of people in the group.

SUPPLIES: slips of paper, pens or pencils, chalkboard or newsprint or dry erase board, chalk or markers

Give each person a slip of paper and a pen or pencil, and instruct players to write their names on their slips of paper. Collect the folded slips and allow players to interact for five minutes, trying to learn as much as they can about others in the group.

SAY:
Each one of you will be given a slip of paper with someone's name on it. You'll have another chance to talk to that person for a few moments. When it's your turn, you'll illustrate clues that will help the other players guess the name you've drawn. You'll have one minute.

Encourage players not to focus on the appearance, but rather on the interests, hobbies, or qualities of the person they're drawing.

To begin, randomly pass out the slips of paper to players, reminding them not to show the papers to anyone. Then give players a few more minutes to talk with each other and learn about the people whose names they drew. Remind players to talk with more than one person, though, to avoid revealing whose names they have.

Allow players to take turns drawing clues on a chalkboard, a dry erase board, or newsprint. Each person should have one minute to draw clues while others try to guess whose name that person drew.

Quick Sort

DESCRIPTION: Teams will race to position themselves in the order suggested.

SUPPLIES: none

Have players form two teams.

SAY:

I'll suggest categories, and each team should sort itself as quickly as possible into a line in the order I've suggested. For example, if I call out, "Sort by age, youngest to oldest," your team should form a line with the youngest person on one end and the oldest on the other.

Before keeping score, try several practice rounds. Then award a point each round to the team that gets in line most quickly. This will call for some rough estimates at times, but teams should be able to defend their positions and orders.

Here are some sorting suggestions to get you started:

- **Sort by height from shortest to tallest.**
- **Sort by shoe size from largest to smallest.**
- **Sort by the number of states you have visited, most states to fewest.**

- Sort by the farthest distance ever traveled, farthest to shortest distance.
- Sort by the number of instruments you play, most to least.
- Sort by the number of times you've moved, least to most.
- Sort by the number of books you've read (not school-related), most to least.
- Sort by the number of siblings you have, least to most.
- Sort by the number of pizza slices you can down at one meal, most to least.
- Sort by the number of times you've been stung by a bee, least to most.
- Sort by the ounces of soda you drink in a day, most to least.
- Sort by the number of Chinese restaurants you've been at, least to most.
- Sort by the number of times you've been carsick, most to least.
- Sort by the number of trees in your yard, least to most.
- Sort by the number of Bible verses you've memorized, most to least.

- **Sort by the number of movies you've been to this year, least to most.**

- **Sort by the number of traffic violations you've had, most to least.**

- **Sort by the number of times you've been in-line skating, least to most.**

- **Sort by the average number of school days you miss(ed) in a year, most to least.**

Rhyming Facts

DESCRIPTION: People will tell about themselves by sharing facts that rhyme with their names.

SUPPLIES: none

Have players form a circle. Explain to the group that participants will share their names and facts about themselves that rhyme with their names. Each person should share one fact. For example, someone might say, "My name is Jim, and 'Amazing Grace' is my favorite hymn."

Play several rounds if possible, seeing how many rhyming facts people can come up with.

Ribbon Pull

DESCRIPTION: Participants will pull colorful ribbons from inside a cake and answer the questions tied to the ribbons.

SUPPLIES: cake, frosting, slips of paper, pen, plastic wrap, ribbons, knife, forks, small plates

Before the game, prepare a cake. When the cake is cool, frost it. (Or if you're short on time or ambition, buy a ready-made cake at your grocery store.) Write questions (see suggestions on page 73) on small slips of paper and roll each question into a tiny scroll. You'll need at least one scroll for each participant. Using plastic wrap, completely cover each scroll.

Tie one end of each scroll to a colorful ribbon. Then push the rolled-up questions into various places in the sides of the cake. The scrolls should be inside the cake, and only the ribbons will be seen. Use extra frosting to completely cover the holes if necessary.

To begin the game, set out the cake and have participants gather around it. Have players take turns selecting a colorful ribbon and gently pulling it from the cake. Once a person removes a ribbon, he or she should open the scroll and read the question written on it. After the player has read the question aloud and answered it, have another player choose a ribbon and pull it out, read the question, and answer it.

Here are some suggested questions to include:

- What is your favorite food?
- What is (or was) your least favorite subject in school?
- What do you like to do on the weekends?
- What is the nicest thing anyone ever said to you?
- Who inspires you to succeed?
- What do you do when you're discouraged?
- If you could visit anywhere in the world, where would you go?
- What do you admire most in your parents?
- Who is your favorite music group and why?

After everyone has pulled a ribbon, cut the cake and enjoy!

Roll a Conversation

DESCRIPTION: This game provides a fun way to start conversations among participants.

SUPPLIES: several small square boxes that can be closed (one for each group of four), newsprint, tape, markers, stopwatch or watch with second hand

Before the game, close the small boxes and wrap each one in newsprint. Then write one of the following questions on each side of each box:

- What's your favorite holiday? Why?
- If you had a million dollars to spend, what would you buy?
- If you could have dinner with anyone, alive or dead, who would it be? Why?
- What's the Bible story that means the most to you? Explain.
- Tell about a special family memory.
- What is your greatest strength?

Have participants form groups of four, and give each group a box.

Game Leader TIP

IF YOU'RE SHORT ON TIME, DON'T CREATE THE CONVERSATION CUBES. INSTEAD, WRITE A NUMBERED LIST OF THE QUESTIONS FOR EACH TEAM AND THEN GIVE EACH TEAM A DIE INSTEAD OF A BOX. TELL TEAMS TO DISCUSS THE QUESTIONS ON THEIR LISTS THAT CORRESPOND WITH THE NUMBERS ON THE DIE.

SAY:

You're going to get to know the people in your group a little better using a "Conversation Cube." Here's how it works: The first thing you'll need to do is have everyone in your group introduce themselves. Then one person in your group will need to "roll" the cube. The question that's on the top when the cube lands is the question everyone in your group will take turns answering. Your group has two minutes to do this. Ready? Go!

After two minutes, have participants mingle and then form new groups of four. Have them repeat the process, giving them two minutes to introduce themselves and answer a question. Continue in this manner until each participant has been in several different groups.

Same Old, Same Old

DESCRIPTION: Participants will get to know each other better by determining a series of things they have in common as a group.

SUPPLIES: newsprint or dry erase board, marker, paper, pens or pencils

Before the game, list the following categories on a piece of newsprint or a dry erase board.

- food
- TV show
- song
- hobby
- sport
- school subject
- game
- way to spend the weekend
- place to visit on vacation
- celebrity

Have participants form groups of five to seven people. Give each group paper and a pen or pencil. Explain that the object of the game is to find one item for each category that everyone in the group agrees that they like and one item in each category that the entire group agrees they dislike. Give them ten minutes to list all their answers. Encourage them to be honest, not to make up their answers in an effort to get points.

Award a point for each response groups come up with.

Shake, Play, and Hug

DESCRIPTION: This game breaks down barriers and helps players get to know each other.

SUPPLIES: none

Have participants form groups of six to eight, but keep the groups evenly numbered if possible. Have each group form a circle.

In each group, one person should walk around the circle counterclockwise, shaking everyone's hand and introducing himself or herself with some creativity. Once a person has shaken everyone's hand, the person to his or her right will do the same thing, and so on until everyone has gone around the circle and shaken everyone's hand.

Game Leader TIP

JUST FOR FUN, TRY HAVING YOUR ENTIRE GROUP LOCK ARMS AND STAND UP TOGETHER. THIS MAKES FOR A LITTLE CHALLENGE, BUT THE STRENGTH OF TEAMWORK MAKES IT POSSIBLE TO STAND UP.

Now the first person goes again, but this time playing some version of Patty-Cake with each person in the circle. Again, encourage players to be creative in playing Patty-Cake. Just as before, the game goes counterclockwise until every person has had a turn to walk around the circle and play.

Once everyone has finished playing Patty-Cake, the first person starts again by gently hugging each person in the circle. Everyone will take a turn hugging each person in the group.

After the group has finished shaking, playing, and hugging, players should form pairs. Partners should stand back to back and sit down with their arms interlocked. Now they must stand up again while keeping their arms interlocked and backs together. Next, put two pairs side by side, and have them lock their arms together while standing back to back with another pair. They must repeat the procedure of sitting down and standing up.

Players should continue adding pairs until the entire group has sat down and stood up together. The first team to complete this entire sequence of events is the winner.

Trivia Scavenger Hunt

DESCRIPTION: Participants will get to know what others know by asking questions in this "scavenger hunt."

SUPPLIES: pens or pencils, index cards

Before the game, write trivia questions on index cards. You'll need three questions on each card, and one card for each participant. Use each question only once. For example, you might ask questions such as "What are the names of three characters from *Sesame Street?*" or "Who was the U.S. president who preceded Lyndon Johnson?" Good sources for trivia questions are games such as Trivial Pursuit or books on trivia and topics like pop culture, sports, or history.

To begin the game, give each person a card and a pen or pencil. Ask players to write their names on the cards. Explain that, as in a scavenger hunt, players must locate items. However, in this game, "items" are the people who possess the answers to the trivia questions on the cards. Players will need to assess the questions to determine who in the room is most likely to know the answer to each question.

When players have acquired answers to their questions, have them sit down. Even after they've completed their cards, others still attempting to find answers may approach them.

When all the cards are completed, each person should announce the answers to their questions, introducing the people who provided them with the knowledge they sought.

What's Your Number?

DESCRIPTION: Players will design license plates to answer several questions, then play a guessing game.

SUPPLIES: poster board, markers, table, paper, pens or pencils

Give each person a piece of poster board and a few markers. Have players spread out so they can't see each other's work.

Explain that each person will create a "vanity license plate" on the poster board. You'll read several questions aloud. After each question, each person must draw a number, letter, or shape on the vanity plate in answer to your question.

Call out five to seven questions such as these:

- **What is your favorite food?**
- **What is your favorite car?**
- **What is your favorite sport?**
- **What is your favorite clothing style?**
- **What is your favorite music group?**
- **What is your favorite book?**
- **What position are you in your family?**
- **How many months until your birthday?**
- **How old are you?**
- **What is your middle name?**
- **What is your nickname?**

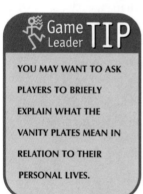

Game Leader TIP

YOU MAY WANT TO ASK PLAYERS TO BRIEFLY EXPLAIN WHAT THE VANITY PLATES MEAN IN RELATION TO THEIR PERSONAL LIVES.

Once you've read all the questions, allow players five minutes to finish their vanity plates. Then gather the finished vanity plates and place them on a table for display. Give each person paper and a pen or pencil. Have each person try to match each vanity plate to the person who designed it, recording guesses on the paper.

Have players reveal who created each vanity plate, then tally the guesses. The person with the most correct guesses wins the game.

SECTION 4

Games With a Point

Anaconda

DESCRIPTION: Participants will team up for a body-twisting race.

SUPPLIES: Bibles

Have participants form teams of about ten to twelve people. Each team should form a single-file line, and teams should stand parallel to each other. Each player should bend over and reach between his or her legs with the right hand, grasping the left hand of the person standing directly behind.

When you shout "go," the person at the back of each line should lie down and the player in front of that person should step backward, straddling the prostrate body of the person behind him or her, then lie down while continuing to hold the hand of the first person to lie down. This continues as players walk over the people behind them and lie down without letting go of their hands. The team that lies down first is the winner. If a team member lets go of someone's hand, that team must start over from the beginning.

The game isn't over until the person originally at the front of the line has lain down. To make the game even more challenging, reverse the game and make the teams stand up again.

After the game, ask these discussion questions:

- **The anaconda swallows its prey without chewing. How does this game remind you of an anaconda?**
- **What are some characteristics of a snake?**
- **Why do you think most people don't like snakes?**
- **Read Genesis 3:4, 13. What did the snake do in these Scriptures?**
- **Who did the snake represent?**
- **Read Proverbs 23:31-33. What is this Scripture talking about?**
- **What does the snake represent in this proverb?**
- **How do the Scriptures in Genesis and Proverbs relate?**
- **Why is the snake such a powerful symbol?**

Balloon Blast

DESCRIPTION: Without using their hands, two teams will compete to see who can blow a balloon to a goal line.

SUPPLIES: Bible, one table for every eight people, chairs, several inflated balloons

Have players form two teams, A and B. Have half of team A and half of team B stand on one side of the table, and the other half of both teams stand on the other side. Then instruct everyone to be seated so members of teams A and B alternate on both sides of the table (no one should be seated directly beside his or her own team member). There should be an equal number of players from both teams on each side. If you have a large group, put more than one table end to end to extend the length. Then instruct players to scoot up close to the table and sit on their hands. Players must remain seated throughout the game. Label one end of the table goal A and the other end goal B.

SAY:

The object of the game is to blow the balloon to your team's goal to win a point. You may not use your hands to move the balloon, only your breath. We'll play until one team scores five points.

Begin the game by dropping a balloon on the middle of the table. Or if you have a large group, put more than one balloon in play at a time. After a team wins, mix up the seating positions and play another round.

Afterward, discuss how easily we can be blown around by the world if we aren't grounded in our faith. Read aloud Ephesians 4:13-14, and ask:

- **How easily did the balloon change directions in the game? Why?**

- **According to the Scripture, how are we like the balloon when we're not mature in our faith?**

- **What kinds of things in the world today might make us change directions easily?**

- **How can we become more mature in our faith?**

Blind Drawings

DESCRIPTION: People will form small groups and attempt to draw a face blindfolded.

SUPPLIES: Bible, paper, pens or pencils, blindfolds

Have people form groups of six. If you have some groups of fewer than six, have some people take more than one turn.

Give each person paper and a pen or pencil. Explain that each group member will draw part of a face while blindfolded. Each group will assign one person each to the mouth, eyes, ears, nose, outline of the face, and hair. Then group members will each take a turn being blindfolded and drawing his or her part of the face. Team members can't help or guide each other to draw.

When teams are finished, have them show each other their group art. Then read aloud Matthew 21:28-32, emphasizing verse 32. Ask:

- **What was difficult about this task?**
- **What would have made the pictures better? Why?**
- **Do you think it would have been easier to put together the whole picture of who Jesus is if you had lived when he walked the earth? Explain.**
- **How can having faith and knowing God is working in your life improve your view of things?**

Blind Sandwich Maker

DESCRIPTION: A blindfolded player will make a sandwich and feed it to another participant with helpful directives from another teammate.

SUPPLIES: ingredients and utensils to make several sandwiches, table, blindfolds

Before the game, set out sandwich-making ingredients and utensils on a table.

Have participants form teams of three. Assign one person in each team to be blindfolded, one to sit quietly somewhere along the edge of the room, and the other to act as a guide.

To begin, each blindfolded partner should go to work making a sandwich. The guides should talk their blindfolded partners through the process, but they may not touch their partners or help them in any other way. When a sandwich is done, the guide should give the blindfolded person verbal directions to help him or her locate their third teammate. When they've reached the third group member, the blindfolded partner should feed that person the sandwich. No one may touch the sandwich but the blindfolded person, and he or she must be guided only by words. The first group to complete all these tasks will win!

After the game,

SAY:

Sometimes we're like blindfolded people. God has given us directions, but we can't see into the future and we feel uncertain. All we can do is trust God's leadership, knowing he has never led us astray.

Ask these questions to trigger discussion:

- **Can you describe a time when you felt worried about the future or uncertain of the outcome of a tricky situation?**

- **What reassurances do we find in the Bible for times like these?**

- **What evidence have you seen in your own life that God is looking out for you?**

Captain Crossing

DESCRIPTION: In a fast-paced manner, members will take turns fulfilling different roles in trios.

SUPPLIES: Bible

Have everyone sit in a circle on the floor. If your group is larger than twelve, have participants form more than one circle. Explain that there are three people to remember in this game—the left oarsman, the right oarsman, and the captain—and that everyone will take turns playing these roles at different times. The left oarsman will pretend to row the boat on the left side of his or her body, the right oarsman will pretend to row the boat on the right side of his or her body, and the captain will sit up straight and hold a salute (raising right hand to forehead). Meanwhile, everyone who isn't fulfilling one of these roles will be clapping his or her hands together continuously.

SAY:

To begin, everyone begins clapping. Then one person is chosen to be the captain, and that person begins making the appropriate gesture. Immediately the people seated to the left and right of the captain become the left and right oarsmen, and they also begin making the appropriate gestures. To play, the captain chooses someone else to be the captain by suddenly stopping the salute and quickly clapping hands so that his or her fingers clearly point to another person in the group. *That* person then immediately becomes the captain, the people to the right and left immediately become the oarsmen, and the former trio disbands and claps with everyone else.

Explain that if anyone displays the wrong gesture at the wrong time or pauses too long before realizing his or her role, the game halts and that person is eliminated before resuming play. The game continues in this fashion until just three people remain.

Afterward, discuss how each person in the body of Christ has a role to fulfill based on the gifts and talents God has given us. Read aloud Romans 12:6-8, and ask:

- **What was difficult about this game?**
- **Why did the roles in this game get confusing?**
- **Why should we seek to discover the roles God has given us to fulfill?**

- **What are some of the roles God calls us to fulfill in the body of Christ?**
- **Can the roles we fulfill for God's church be demonstrated as clearly as the different roles in this game were? Why or why not?**

Compass Journey

DESCRIPTION: Participants will use a compass to take a journey together.

SUPPLIES: paper, pen or pencil, compass for each group of five to eight, end-of-trail marker, photocopies of typed instructions

Before the game, plot out a compass course outside, preferably in a large area. To do this, mark a beginning point, hold a compass in your hand, and step off any number of paces, keeping track of your direction. As you create your journey, record the number of paces you make on a piece of paper and record the changes of direction you make at certain points. Place a marker at the end of your course.

After you've plotted your course, type up the instructions and make a copy for each group of five to eight.

To begin the game, have participants form groups of five to eight people. Give each group a compass and a copy of your instructions. Then send the groups out in five-minute intervals. See if the groups can make the same journey you did and locate your marker.

Once everyone has taken the journey, gather as a large group and ask these questions:

- **In what ways was this journey difficult? easy?**
- **How were the instruction sheet and the compass helpful? What wasn't helpful about them?**
- **What kinds of instructions can help us with our journey through life?**
- **Who or what do people look to as their compasses in life?**
- **Where do you look for your compass in life?**
- **How does it help to have a guide on our journey through life?**

Dental Scripting

DESCRIPTION: Participants will draw pictures with their teeth.

SUPPLIES: newsprint, tape, new pencils, photocopies of the picture on page 88

Before the game, hang two sheets of newsprint at one end of the meeting area. Be sure to hang the newsprint about face-high on the wall so participants can easily draw a picture on it using their teeth. Make two enlarged photocopies of the picture on page 88.

Have participants form two teams. Give each person a pencil.

SAY:
Today your art skills are going to be put to the test. I'm going to ask your group to draw a picture. Before we begin, I'd like to show you the picture.

Give each group a photocopy of the picture on page 88.

When they're ready, give groups the signal to begin. Call time every ten seconds until every team member has had a chance to draw. When everyone has drawn something on the paper, stop the game. Have everyone gather at the drawings, and congratulate everyone's effort.

Have teams break up to form groups of four. Have groups discuss the following questions:

Game Leader TIP

HAVE STUDENTS THROW THEIR PENCILS AWAY WHEN THE GAME IS FINISHED.

- **What made this game difficult? Why?**
- **How was this activity like situations that cause you stress? How was it different?**
- **What are some good ways to deal with stress?**

Distinctly Designed

DESCRIPTION: Group members will try to discover a mystery person among them by asking yes-or-no questions.

SUPPLIES: Bible

Have players sit in a circle on the floor. If your group is larger than twenty, have players form more than one circle. Choose one person to be the Answer Person. Have everyone else hide their eyes. Instruct the Answer Person to walk around the outside of the circle, tapping everyone on the back once except for one person, whom he or she should tap twice. This person will be the Mystery Person for that round. Then have the Answer Person sit down in the middle of the circle.

SAY:

One of you was tapped twice on the back instead of just once. You are our Mystery Person. The goal of this game is to determine the identity of the Mystery Person by asking the Answer Person in the middle yes-or-no questions, such as "Does the mystery person have brown hair?" "Does the mystery person like volleyball?" and so on. If you're the Mystery Person, you should participate in asking questions also so you don't reveal who you are by not participating.

Let everyone in the circle take turns asking questions until there is a group consensus on who the Mystery Person is. Play several rounds, so everyone in the circle has a chance to be either the Answer Person or the Mystery Person.

Afterward, discuss how each member of your group is special and was created unique by God. Read aloud Psalm 139:13-16, and ask:

- **What made finding the Mystery Person easy or difficult?**

- **What are some key characteristics that distinguished one person from another?**

- **What does this Scripture say regarding our individuality?**

- **How does this Scripture make you feel about yourself?**

Harvest Trip-Up

DESCRIPTION: This game requires a little skill to reach the finish line.

SUPPLIES: Bible, two buckets of water

Have participants form two teams, and split each team into two even sections, keeping four people from each team available as runners. Have each section form a line opposite the other section of their team, and have them sit on the floor facing each other with the soles of their feet together. Each section should sit at least an outstretched arm's length apart in their line.

Keeping the soles of their feet together, players should spread their legs apart so that the feet of the people on both sides should be touching theirs. Now they should sweep their legs in and out slowly, as they keep their soles together, like a pair of scissors.

The four people selected as the runners should stand at the ends of the sitting line, two people standing at each end. As teammates sweep their legs back and forth slowly, the runners must carefully run through their legs one at a time, while carrying a bucket of water, without being clipped by the

legs as they close in and out. Their goal is to reach the runner waiting on the opposite end of the line without being clipped. The waiting runner will take the bucket and carry it back to the runner waiting on the opposite end until all four have had a turn. In other words, they'll do a relay with the bucket as they run between the legs of their teammates.

If a runner is hit by the leg of a teammate, he or she must go back to the beginning of the line and start over. The winning team is the one that has successfully passed the bucket from one end to the other and has the most water still in the bucket after all four have had a turn.

After the game, ask these questions to spark discussion:

- **What was it like to carry the bucket while running and trying to avoid obstacles?**
- **How were the obstacles in this game similar to the difficulties of trying to harvest a crop or tend a garden?**
- **How does this game remind you of harvesting crops?**
- **How was the water in this game similar to water used in harvesting? How was it different?**

Read Matthew 9:37 aloud. Ask:

- **What did Jesus mean when he said, "The harvest is plentiful but the workers are few"?**
- **Paul said in 1 Corinthians 3:6, "I planted the seed, Apollos watered it, but God made it grow." What did he mean?**
- **How can you plant or water a seed in someone's life?**
- **What does it take for a "seed" to grow into new faith?**

Hat Elimination

DESCRIPTION: Participants will exchange hats quickly and will learn the value of including everyone.

SUPPLIES: one hat for each person

You may want to save this game for the end of a meeting when players don't mind messing up their hair!

Ask players to stand in a circle. If your group is large, you may want to divide into several groups for this game, and have each group form a circle.

Give everyone in the circle a hat. To begin the game, instruct the group to begin passing the hats to the left. Each person will remove the hat from his or her own head and place it on the head of the person to the left. Of course, as each person is doing this, he or she is receiving a new hat from the person to the right. Practice this for a few rounds and see how quickly the group can pass the hats.

Once the group has mastered the technique, remove a hat from the circle. Have players continue passing the hats as before. When you say "stop," the person without a hat must leave the group. Continue removing a hat each round until only one person remains.

Then ask these questions to start a discussion about including others:

- **What different kinds of "hats" do people wear in real life?**
- **What did it feel like to be included in the group?**
- **What did it feel like to be excluded from the group?**
- **What are some ways we exclude others in our activities and social circles?**
- **Why do you think people tend to exclude others?**
- **What are some things we can do to make people feel more welcome in our groups?**

It's a Draw

DESCRIPTION: This game will emphasize the need for clear communication.

SUPPLIES: newsprint, markers, pictures (from magazines or elsewhere), stopwatch or watch with second hand

Have participants form pairs. If this is a family event, you might want to pair off parents and young people. Give each pair a piece of newsprint and a marker.

Explain that pairs will have sixty seconds to complete a drawing. You'll display a picture, and one player in each pair will tell the other what to draw. Partners may not look at each other. The player giving the instructions may not use hand motions and may not tell what the picture is. The instructing player may only describe how to draw the picture.

Have drawing players get ready to draw while their partners stand behind them.

Show instructing players a picture of a popular cartoon character, a famous painting, food, or some other image. Say "go," and give players sixty seconds to draw as their partners instruct them. Then call time and compare what was drawn with the original picture. Then have partners switch places and start again with a new picture.

You can give a prize to the team that comes the closest to the original images, but it may be easier to declare a "draw."

After the game, initiate a discussion by asking these questions:

- **What was most difficult about being the artist? Why?**

- **What was most difficult about being the instructor? Why?**

- **As you explained how to draw the picture, what did you do to make your point as clear as possible?**

- **As the artist, why was it sometimes hard to understand what was expected of you?**

- **What are some things that make communication easier?**

- **What are some things that hinder communication?**

- **What happens when the end result is not what you expected?**

- **How is this game like relationships between parents and their children?**

Leading the Blind

DESCRIPTION: Players will take turns guiding their blindfolded partners to create an object.

SUPPLIES: Bible, one small paper lunch sack for each person, marker, craft sticks, glue or tape, yarn, scissors, O-shaped cereal, one blindfold for every two people

Before the game, label half the paper sacks "A" and the other half "B." In each A sack, place four craft sticks and either a roll of tape or a bottle of glue. In each B sack, place a piece of yarn three feet long and ten pieces of O-shaped cereal.

Create a sample of object A by gluing or taping four craft sticks together to form a cross. Create a sample of object B by stringing together ten pieces of cereal on yarn to create a cereal "necklace." Set these samples aside where no one will see them.

Have players form pairs. Give each pair a blindfold, one paper sack A, and one paper sack B. Don't allow players to look in the sacks yet. Explain that whoever wears the blindfold will be making something with his or her hands by relying on the partner's instructions. The nonblindfolded partners will be shown an object, and it's their job to guide their partners in making that object. Partners can communicate freely, but the one giving instructions cannot use his or her hands or touch the materials in any way, and the blindfolded person cannot peek at any time.

To begin, have one partner from each pair securely blindfold the other and set paper sack A directly in front of him or her (keep paper sack B set aside). Then show all the nonblindfolded members object A, a cross made from four craft sticks glued or taped together.

SAY:
Blindfolded members, you may open your sacks and begin.

After five minutes, instruct players to stop. Then have partners switch roles, using paper sack B and displaying object B, a cereal "necklace." Allow five minutes for this project also.

Afterward, discuss how important it was for blindfolded members to rely on their partners' voices to guide them. Read John 16:13 aloud, and ask:

- **How did it feel when you were dependent upon your partner to guide your hands?**

- **How is being blindfolded in this game like walking by faith?**

- **How is listening to your partner's voice like listening for the Spirit's voice to guide you?**

- **How can we learn to build our faith and rely more fully on the Holy Spirit's guidance in our lives?**

Mind Meld

DESCRIPTION: Participants will write lists of words beginning with a certain letter, hoping to make matches with the words on their partners' lists.

SUPPLIES: Bible, paper, pens or pencils, stopwatch or watch with second hand

Distribute paper and pens or pencils to all players, and ask each person to find a partner.

SAY:

I'll give you a letter of the alphabet and you'll have thirty seconds to write down words beginning with that letter. At the end of that time, you'll compare your list with your partner's list and receive five points for every word that appears on both lists.

Announce a letter of your choice and begin. Continue for several rounds, choosing a new letter of the alphabet each time.

After the game,

SAY:

It must have been difficult trying to anticipate what your partner might write down, even if you know each other pretty well. None of us can read minds, but the Bible does encourage us to be "like-minded."

Read Philippians 2:1-4 aloud.

Ask:

- **What does it mean to be like-minded?**

- **How can we achieve this kind of unity?**

- **What do humility and unselfishness have to do with unity?**

- **What did Christ's example of unselfishness look like?**

- **What can we do to become more united? more unselfish in our relationships?**

Nuclear Family

DESCRIPTION: Groups will put together perfect families.

SUPPLIES: Bible, poster board or newsprint, lots of magazines, scissors, glue sticks

Have participants form groups of four to six. If this is a family event, have each family form a group. Give each group a piece of poster board or newsprint, a stack of magazines, scissors, and a glue stick.

Explain that each group is going to create the "perfect nuclear family." Each poster will contain a mom, a dad, a daughter, a son, and a pet. Each member of the family must have a full face (eyes, nose, ears, mouth, hair) and a full body (torso, legs, feet, arms, hands). Here's the catch: No two pieces can come from the same picture in a magazine. Size and shape does not have to be consistent.

The first group to complete its "nuclear family" is the winner. You can award prizes for scariest or funniest collage, or think of your own categories.

Ask:

- **Why do people sometimes portray "mom, dad, sister, brother, pet" as the ideal family?**

- **What is an ideal family?**

- **How has our culture's view of family changed over recent decades? Why?**

- **How have television and other media affected our view of what "family" means?**

- **What do you like most about your family?**

- **In what ways could your family be strengthened?**

Read the following Scriptures aloud, or have volunteers read them: Proverbs 10:1; Ephesians 6:1-4; 1 Timothy 5:8. Ask:

- **What does the Bible say about family?**

- **What one thing could you personally do to strengthen your family?**

Orange Puzzles

DESCRIPTION: Participants will work together to reapply orange peels.

SUPPLIES: one orange and one bottle of glue for each group of four to six

Have participants form groups of four to six people. Give each group an orange. Instruct groups to peel their oranges, being sure to keep all the peel.

When groups have peeled their oranges, have each group place their orange peels in a pile and put their peeled orange next to the peels.

SAY:
I've got a challenge for you. I'd like you to find an orange pile that's not yours. When I give the signal, work together to see which group can put their peels back on their orange so all the peels fit in the right places. Use the glue to keep the peel in its place.

Give groups glue, and signal for them to begin. When they're finished, congratulate the winning group and applaud everyone's effort.

Have groups discuss the following questions:

- **When have you felt like life was falling apart?**

- **When have you tried to put a situation back together? What was that like?**

- **What in your life serves as the glue to keep things together?**

- **When has God helped or strengthened you during a tough time in your life?**

Pick a Family

DESCRIPTION: Adults and young people will learn more about each other by asking probing questions in this provocative game.

SUPPLIES: index cards, pens or pencils, partition, chairs

Have participants form two teams: adults and young people. Explain that this game is like *The Dating Game*. Players will have a chance to interview others, assess their qualifications, and choose family members for themselves. Give each person an index card and a pen or pencil. Ask each player to write down at least one question he or she would like to ask people on the other team. For example, a teenager might write, "If I were going out with my friends on Friday night, what time would you require me to be back home?" An adult might write, "If I allowed you to drive your friends in the family car, how would you demonstrate responsibility?"

Once all players have written their questions, place three young people or three adults behind a screen or partition and invite someone from the other group to "interview" them, making sure no one will actually be interviewing his or her own family member. Allow players to interview contestants and choose family members for themselves.

After the game, ask these discussion questions:

- **What did you learn about being an adult? a young person?**

- **What questions were particularly thought-provoking during this game?**

- **How might adults and young people communicate more effectively?**

- **How might this game help you be a more understanding family member?**

Putting the Pieces Together

DESCRIPTION: Participants will need to work together to find all the puzzle pieces.

SUPPLIES: Bible, children's puzzles with the same number of pieces in each puzzle, marker

Before the game, find several families in your church who are willing to be home for the evening and to be part of this scavenger hunt. Write the following information on the backs of the pieces to each puzzle: names of the families in your church that will be part of the scavenger hunt and a letter code for a particular team. For example, if the puzzle has eight pieces, you'll write the names of seven different families on the backs of the pieces, one name per piece. You'll also write the name of the starting point on the eighth puzzle piece. On each piece of that puzzle, you'll also write the letter A for team A.

Give each participating family one puzzle piece from each puzzle. Those puzzle pieces will indicate to teams where they're supposed to go next. In advance, you'll have to figure out which pieces of the puzzles go to which families, depending on the order you want the various teams to travel. The last piece of the puzzle should direct the group back to the starting point.

Each family should also receive instructions to give to the teams who come to their homes. Give each family one instruction they'll ask each group to perform. Here are some suggestions for instructions:

- Tell two good, clean jokes to the family who lives in this home.

- Run three laps around the outside of the house.

- Make a circle and sing a hymn.

- Recite your favorite passage of Scripture (or one you all can remember).

- Hug everyone who lives in this home.

- Donate all your pocket change to the family at this home.

- Sit down and share a funny experience with the family.

Have participants form teams, one for each puzzle you have. Assign each team a letter that matches a puzzle you've prepared. Give each team its first puzzle piece with the name of a church family on the back (each team should start at a different home).

Explain that teams will need to go to those homes, where they'll be given instructions by the families. They'll need to follow those instructions in order to get their next puzzle piece. The next piece will tell them where to go next. The group that arrives back at the starting point first with their puzzle complete is the winner.

After the game, talk about what it means to encourage each other in the body of Christ. Read Philippians 2:1-2, and ask:

- **What does it mean to be united?**
- **What is the most difficult part of encouraging, comforting, and supporting others in the church?**
- **What are some ways we can show compassion and fellowship to each other?**
- **Is it easier for you to have fun with and show affection for family members or with friends and others outside your family? Explain.**

Seeing Jesus

DESCRIPTION: Participants will understand what it means to see Jesus in the "less fortunate" of their world.

SUPPLIES: Bible, small boxes of crackers, blindfolds, large bandages, coats and hats, paper cups, pitcher of drinking water

Before the game, set up five stations in your meeting area. Spread out the stations as much as you can. At station one, place small boxes of crackers. Put blindfolds at station two and bandages at station three. At station four, place coats and hats. And at station five, set out paper cups and a pitcher of drinking water.

Have participants form teams of at least six. If teams aren't equal, some team members will have to go more than once. Explain that each person on the team will be part of a relay. One person on each team should be stationed at each of the five stations. The remaining people on the team will be the runners, going from station to station.

At the first station, a team member will feed the runner an entire box of crackers. Then the runner should proceed to the next station, where another member of the team will blindfold the runner and lead him or her to the third station. When they get to the third station, another member of the team will wrap the runner with a bandage. Since the runner is now blindfolded and wrapped in a bandage, he or she will need to be guided to the next station, where a member of the team will help him or her put on a coat and hat. Finally, the runner will proceed to station five, where a team member will pour a cup of water and hold it so the runner can drink the entire thing.

The first team to have all its runners complete all the stations wins.

After the game, discuss how each member of the team had a role in helping the runner. Read Matthew 25:31-46, and ask:

- **What do you think each action in the game represented?**
- **What was the most difficult part of this game?**
- **Why is it often difficult to help people in need in our world?**
- **What things can we do to be more sensitive to the needs of those around us?**
- **How can we "see Jesus" in people who are in need?**

Sew Expressive

DESCRIPTION: Teams will sew felt facial and body features to make complete bodies.

SUPPLIES: Bibles, felt squares, felt scraps, fine-tip markers, scissors, needles, thread, newsprint or a dry erase board, marker

Have players form teams of three. If necessary, create some teams of four. Give each team a felt square, felt scraps, a fine-tip marker, a Bible, scissors, a needle, and thread.

Read 1 Corinthians 12:12-26 aloud, then write the following body parts from this passage on newsprint or a dry erase board: foot, hand, ear, eye, and head.

Tell teams to get ready to create the "perfect body" by cutting out the body parts listed above and quickly sewing them onto the felt backing. As one player cuts out felt body parts, another should be sewing them onto the felt square. A third team member should be busy looking for verses that define how we should use each body part. For example, a person may identify Matthew 28:18-20 as a description of how we should use our feet: to go where people need to hear the good news about Jesus. Once the third team member locates a descriptive verse, he or she should write the Scripture reference on the felt body part it pertains to. If you have some teams of four, have one person look up verses and another write them on the body parts.

The first team to complete its "body" wins.

After the game, use the following questions to start discussion:

- **What did Paul want us to understand about being part of the body of Christ?**

- **How can we learn to use our individual gifts to complete the body of Christ?**

- **How did this game encourage the principle of each person doing the task which best suits his or her gifts or talents?**

- **When we work as team (or as a body), how are we more effective for Christ than if we try to do everything on our own?**

- **What are some ways we can discover the special gifts God has given us?**

Show Your Fruit

DESCRIPTION: Participants will pantomime the fruits of the Spirit.

SUPPLIES: Bible, paper, pens or pencils

Before this game, write each type of "fruit" from Galatians 5:22-23 on a separate sheet of paper (one paper for each person). You can repeat types of fruit if you have more than nine participants.

Give each person a pen or pencil. Read Galatians 5:22-23 aloud. Ask:

- **Why are these things important?**
- **What are some ways people might exhibit the fruit of the Spirit?**

SAY:

In a moment, I'm going to assign each of you one of these fruits. When you get your paper with your assignment on it, don't show anybody. What I'd like you to do first is think of some ways people might demonstrate your fruit in their lives. If you'd like, make some notes on the paper.

Give each person a piece of paper with a type of spiritual fruit listed on it. Give participants a few moments to think of ways people might demonstrate fruit in their lives.

SAY:

Now I'd like you to look over your notes and think of an easy, clear way you might pantomime your fruit to get someone else to guess what it is. For example, if your fruit is love, you might fold your arms across your chest as if you're giving a big hug.

Give participants a few moments to think.

SAY:

OK, now your goal is to get as many people as possible to guess what your fruit is without talking. Here's how this works: You'll mingle around with other participants and show them your pantomime. You can only show someone your pantomime once. If he or she guesses correctly, have him or her sign your paper. Try to show your pantomime to everyone in the group in the next ten minutes. Remember—no talking, except to guess what others are pantomiming!

Encourage participants to mingle and share their pantomimes. At the end of ten minutes, have participants sit down. Ask:

- **How many people guessed your fruit?**
- **Was it easy or difficult to guess what others were pantomiming? Explain.**

- **Was it easy or difficult to get other people to guess what you were pantomiming? Explain.**
- **How is this experience like demonstrating the fruit of the Spirit in your own life?**
- **Why is it important to show the fruit of the Spirit?**
- **What fruit do you think you demonstrate well? What fruit would you like to work on?**

Sign of the Times

DESCRIPTION: In this intergenerational game, participants will try to fill in a handout that requires them to ask questions of people in different generations.

SUPPLIES: photocopies of the "Times Questionnaire" handout (p. 105), pens or pencils

Give each person a photocopy of the "Times Questionnaire" handout (p. 105) and a pen or pencil. Explain to participants that they should fill in as many boxes as possible. In order to get the answers, they have to ask other players. When they get answers to the questions, they should write down the answers, along with the names of the people who gave them the answers.

After a while, call time and find out who filled in the most boxes. Have that person share his or her answers.

After the game, spark discussion with these questions:

- **Would you have been able to answer all these questions on your own? Why or why not?**
- **Would you have been able to work with people just your age to answer all these questions? Why or why not?**
- **Do you often find yourself receiving knowledge from people older or younger than you? Why or why not?**
- **What is the benefit of learning from people of different ages?**
- **What happens if we disregard people older or younger than us?**
- **What are ways we can learn from people in other generations?**

Times Questionnaire

- **Who was president in 1930?**
  Answer:
  Who Gave You this Answer:

- **Who was president in 1950?**
  Answer:
  Who Gave You this Answer:

- **Who was president in 1970?**
  Answer:
  Who Gave You this Answer:

- **Who is president now?**
  Answer:
  Who Gave You this Answer:

- **Name a popular singer among young people in the 1950s.**
  Answer:
  Who Gave You this Answer:

- **Name a popular singer among young people in the 1970s.**
  Answer:
  Who Gave You this Answer:

- **Name a popular singer among young people in the 1980s.**
  Answer:
  Who Gave You this Answer:

- **Name a popular singer among young people now.**
  Answer:
  Who Gave You this Answer:

- **What was a trendy expression in the 1960s?**
  Answer:
  Who Gave You this Answer:

- **What was a trendy expression in the 1970s?**
  Answer:
  Who Gave You this Answer:

- **What was a trendy expression in the 1980s?**
  Answer:
  Who Gave You this Answer:

- **What's a trendy expression now?**
  Answer:
  Who Gave You this Answer:

- **Who did young people look up to in the 1950s?**
  Answer:
  Who Gave You this Answer:

- **Who did young people look up to in the 1960s?**
  Answer:
  Who Gave You this Answer:

- **Who did young people look up to in the 1970s?**
  Answer:
  Who Gave You this Answer:

- **Who do young people look up to now?**
  Answer:
  Who Gave You this Answer:

- **What was a common fashion trend in the 1950s?**
  Answer:
  Who Gave You this Answer:

- **What was a common fashion trend in the 1970s?**
  Answer:
  Who Gave You this Answer:

- **What was a common fashion trend in the 1980s?**
  Answer:
  Who Gave You this Answer:

- **What's a common fashion trend now?**
  Answer:
  Who Gave You this Answer:

Three to Get Ready...

DESCRIPTION: Teams will face off in a juice-squeezing contest.

SUPPLIES: Bible, chef hats (real or improvised paper ones), aprons, soap, water, towels, knives, oranges, small drinking glasses or paper cups

Have participants form teams of three. Give each team a chef hat, an apron, soap, a towel, a knife, several oranges, and a drinking glass.

Explain that one player on each team will race to prepare a second player to be the chef by placing the chef's hat on his or her head, tying on the apron, and helping the person wash and dry his or her hands. The third teammate will cut the oranges in half and place them near the chef. The chef will be responsible for squeezing the juice of the oranges into the drinking glass until the juice reaches the brim of the glass. The first team to squeeze enough juice to fill the glass wins.

After the game, read James 3:3-12 aloud. Then discuss the following questions:

IT'S A GOOD IDEA TO SAVE THE SQUEEZED ORANGES, OFFERING THEM TO ANYONE WHO NEEDS COMPOST FOR A GARDEN.

- **In what ways do we prepare our hearts and minds to speak in a Christ-honoring way, as our teams prepared their chefs?**

- **How can we resist the squeeze and pressure of the temptation to say things we know are wrong?**

- **How can we discipline ourselves to keep quiet tongues, even when we're under pressure?**

- **How can we work together with friends to challenge each other to Christlike speech?**

Ultimate Cookie Catch

DESCRIPTION: Participants will catch cookies in their mouths (or in cups), trying to score five hundred points.

SUPPLIES: Bible, cookies, paper cups, milk

Ask participants to stand in a cluster in a large open area. Toss cookies into the air, awarding one hundred points each time a person catches a cookie in his or her mouth. If younger children are playing, distribute paper cups that players can use to catch the cookies.

The person to first reach five hundred points will be the winner and will enjoy the distinction of being most likely to have spoiled his or her appetite.

After the game,

SAY:
There's nothing like cookies to make a person thirsty for a glass of milk.

Distribute cups and milk.

Read 1 Peter 2:2-3 aloud and ask:

- **In these verses, what is meant by "pure spiritual milk"?**
- **What would you consider a well-balanced spiritual diet?**
- **In what ways have you found the Lord to be good?**

Unique Ingredients

DESCRIPTION: Participants will share personal insights regarding God's gifts.

SUPPLIES: product ingredient label, pens or pencils, index cards

Read aloud an ingredient label from a common product such as cookies or hot dogs, and challenge participants to guess the identity of the product. After the product has been identified, give each person a pen or pencil and two index cards.

Explain that everyone should write his or her own personal ingredient label on one index card. The list of ingredients should include the person's skills and abilities, personality traits, and so on. Each person should then place an asterisk beside the one trait he or she thinks would most easily reveal the person's identity to the rest of the group. Players should write their names on the cards.

When everyone is finished, collect the ingredient label cards. Have participants number their other cards with the number of participants.

Read through the ingredient labels, highlighting the traits marked by asterisks. As you read, participants should write the name of the person they think wrote each card.

Read through the cards again, identifying the owner of each card. Tally scores and see how well participants know each other.

After the game, follow up with these questions:

- **What do you find most interesting about the variety of skills, talents, and traits listed on these cards?**

- **Why did God create us each with unique combinations of gifts and skills?**

- **How do you think your own particular combination of gifts and skills is suited for things God is asking you to do or become?**

What's in a Name?

DESCRIPTION: Participants will form full-name acrostics based on information shared by others.

SUPPLIES: Bible, paper, pens or pencils

Give each person paper and a pen or pencil. Ask that everyone write his or her full name (first, middle, and last) down the left side of the paper.

Explain that participants are going to walk around the room and try to fill their papers with adjectives from other players. Players should approach each other and pay each other compliments, such as "You're a good friend" or "You have a great smile!"

When a person shares a compliment, the person receiving the compliment should write a positive adjective about the other person by any one letter of that person's name. For example, if Lucy pays a compliment to Scott, Scott might write "courageous" by the C in Lucy's name.

Players need not fill their papers in the order the letters appear in their names, but every letter must be used. Point out that it may be more difficult to find adjectives for some letters than for others. Players may create adjectives, but the words must make sense to everyone else.

When a player has successfully filled his or her paper, he or she must continue to help others finish the game.

When everyone has finished, have players sit in a circle and ask volunteers to share their acrostics. Then start a discussion by asking questions such as these:

- **What was frustrating about this game? What was rewarding?**
- **How did it feel to receive compliments?**
- **How did it feel to share positives?**

Read aloud Ephesians 4:29 and 1 Thessalonians 5:11, and ask:

- **What happens when we share encouraging words?**
- **What happens when we share harmful words?**
- **What can we do to make sure our words are positive?**

Group Publishing, Inc.
Attention: Product Development
P.O. Box 481
Loveland, CO 80539
Fax: (970) 679-4370

Evaluation for
Games for All Ages

Please help Group Publishing, Inc. continue to provide innovative and useful resources for ministry. Please take a moment to fill out this evaluation and mail or fax it to us. Thanks!

● ● ●

1. As a whole, this book has been (circle one)

not very helpful   very helpful

1   2   3   4   5   6   7   8   9   10

2. The best things about this book:

3. Ways this book could be improved:

4. Things I will change because of this book:

5. Other books I'd like to see Group publish in the future:

6. Would you be interested in field-testing future Group products and giving us your feedback? If so, please fill in the information below:

Name_____

Church Name _____

Denomination _____ Church Size _____

Church Address _____

City _____ State _____ ZIP _____

Church Phone _____

E-mail _____

Exciting Resources for Your Youth Ministry

At Risk: Bringing Hope to Hurting Teenagers

Dr. Scott Larson

Discover how to meet the needs of hurting teenagers with these practical suggestions, honest answers, and tools to help you evaluate your existing programs. Plus, you'll get real-life insights about what it takes to include kids others have left behind. If you believe the Gospel is for everyone, this book is for you! Includes a special introduction by Duffy Robbins and a foreword by Dean Borgman.

ISBN 0-7644-2091-7

All-Star Games From All-Star Youth Leaders

The ultimate game book—from the biggest names in youth ministry! All-time no-fail favorites from Wayne Rice, Les Christie, Rich Mullins, Tiger McLuen, Darrell Pearson, Dave Stone, Bart Campolo, Steve Fitzhugh, and 21 others! You get all the games you'll need for any situation. Plus, you get practical advice about how to design your own games and tricks for turning a *good* game into a *great* game!

ISBN 0-7644-2020-8

The Youth Worker's Encyclopedia of Bible-Teaching Ideas

Here are the most comprehensive idea books available for youth workers. With more than 365 creative ideas in each of these 400-page encyclopedias, there's at least one idea for every book of the Bible. You'll find ideas for retreats and overnighters...learning games...adventures...projects...affirmations... parties... prayers... music...devotions...skits...and more!

Old Testament	ISBN 1-55945-184-X
New Testament	ISBN 1-55945-183-1

Awesome Worship Services for Youth

These 12 complete worship services involve kids in 4 key elements of worship: celebration, reflection, symbolic action, and declaration of God's Truth. Flexible and dynamic services each last about an hour and will bring your group closer to God.

ISBN 0-7644-2057-7

More Resources for Your Youth Ministry

New Directions for Youth Ministry
Wayne Rice, Chap Clark and others

Discover ministry strategies and models that are working in *real* churches...with *real* kids. Readers get practical help evaluating what will work in their ministries and a candid look at the pros and cons of implementing each strategy.

ISBN 0-7644-2103-4

Hilarious Skits for Youth Ministry
Chris Chapman

Easy-to-act and fun-to-watch, these 8 youth group skits are guaranteed to get your kids laughing—and listening. These skits help your kids discover spiritual truths! They last from 5 to 15 minutes, so there's a skit to fit into any program!

ISBN 0-7644-2033-X

Character Counts!: 40 Youth Ministry Devotions From Extraordinary Christians
Karl Leuthauser

Inspire your kids, introduce them to authentic heroes, and help them celebrate their heritage of faith with these 40 youth ministry devotions from the lives of extraordinary Christians. These brief, interactive devotions provide powerful testimonies from faithful Christians like Corrie ten Boom, Mother Teresa, Dietrich Bonhoeffer, and Harriet Tubman. Men and women who lived their faith without compromise, demonstrated Christlike character, and whose true stories inspire teenagers to do the same!

ISBN 0-7644-2075-5

On-the-Edge Games for Youth Ministry
Karl Rohnke

Author Karl Rohnke is a recognized, established game guru, and he's packed this book with quality, cooperative, communication-building, brain-stretching, crowdbreaking, flexible, can't-wait-to-try-them games youth leaders love. Readers can tie in these games to Bible-learning opportunities or just play them.

ISBN 0-7644-2058-5